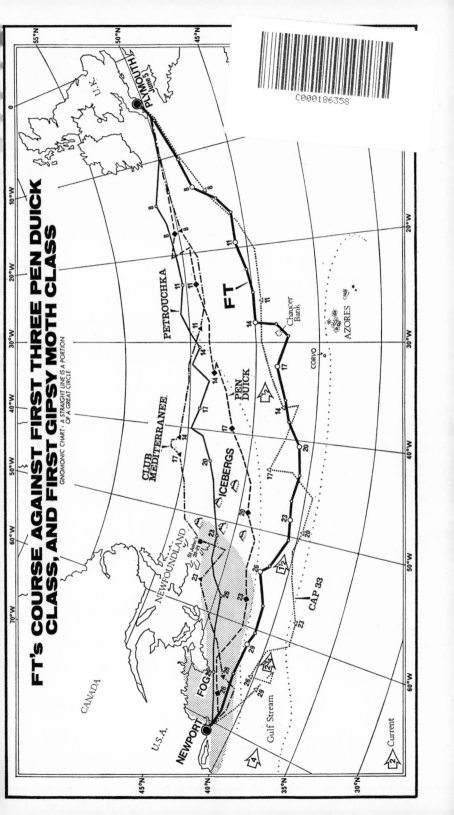

FT's COURSE AGAINST FIRST THREE PEN DUICK CLASS, AND FIRST GIPSY MOTH CLASS

GNOMONIC CHART : A STRAIGHT LINE IS A PORTION OF A GREAT CIRCLE

THE ATLANTIC CHALLENGE
The Story of Trimaran *FT*

THE
ATLANTIC
CHALLENGE

The Story of Trimaran *FT*

DAVID PALMER

HOLLIS & CARTER
LONDON   SYDNEY
TORONTO

© David Palmer 1977
ISBN 0 370 30031 9
Printed in Great Britain for
Hollis & Carter
an associate company of
The Bodley Head Ltd
9 Bow Street, London WC2E 7AL
by W & J Mackay Limited, Chatham
Set in Baskerville
First published 1977

To Elizabeth and James

CONTENTS

LINE ILLUSTRATIONS

Courses of first five, *Jester* class;
FT's course against first three *Pen Duick* class,
and first *Gipsy Moth* class, *endpapers*

The charts were drawn by Martyn Barnes,
the Appendix illustrations by Elizabeth Palmer.

LIST OF PLATES

ACKNOWLEDGMENTS

The *FT* project at one time or another involved literally hundreds of people, to every one of whom the writing of this book represents a heartfelt thank you. I wish to thank in particular Lord Drogheda, whose enthusiastic support for my plans ensured the backing of the *Financial Times*; Fredy Fisher, my editor, for his great tolerance in the face of long absences; Alan Hare, the paper's chief executive, for his support; Justin Dukes, joint general manager, for much help and good advice; and Tony Moreton, deputy news editor, who never once complained, although he had plenty of reason to.

Derek Kelsall, who designed and built *FT*; Peter Dove of Hood Sailmakers, who gave her the best suit of sails in the multi-hull fleet; Terry Pearce of International Yacht Equipment, whose spars never gave any trouble; Luke FitzHerbert, who contributed so much to *FT* throughout the design period and during her first season; and Ralph Farrant for giving me my first sail in a trimaran, and for his fatherly interest in *FT*.

I am also grateful to Glyn Genin, Freddie Mansfield, Trevor Humphries, Terry Kirk and Ashley Ashwood of the *Financial Times* pictures department for the many photographs they took, including the majority of those in this book; to Martyn Barnes, head of the *Financial Times* cartography department, who is responsible for all the charts; and to David Carrick, the *Financial Times* doctor, for his invaluable help on medical provisions.

Most of all, I have to thank my father, who taught me to sail; and my wife, who put up with it all for four years, and who has done many of the illustrations for this book.

David Palmer
May, 1977

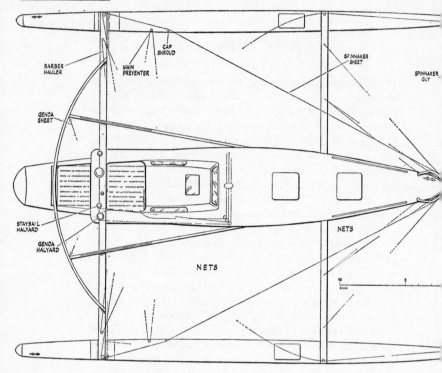

BARBER
HAULER

MAIN
PREVENTER

CAP
SHROUD

SPINNAKER
SHEET

SPINNAKER
GUY

GENOA
SHEET

STAYSAIL
HALYARD

GENOA
HALYARD

NETS

NETS

10   5
Scale

NETS

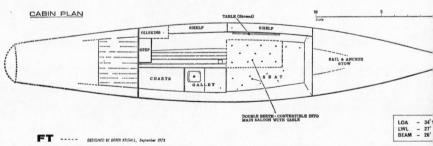

CABIN PLAN

TABLE (Stowed)

OILSKINS   SHELF   SHELF

STEP

SAIL & ANCHOR
STOW

CHARTS   GALLEY   SEAT

DOUBLE BERTH - CONVERTIBLE INTO
MAIN SALOON WITH TABLE

10   5
Scale

FT ----   DESIGNED BY DEREK KELSALL, September 1973

LOA – 34'
LWL – 27'
BEAM – 26'

1 General arrangement drawing.

I

THE FOG

The fog comes in in the middle of the night. One minute I am on *FT*'s deck, keeping an eye on the lights of half a dozen trawlers that have hove into view from various directions; the next, I am blindfold, peering into the dank darkness, listening for the sound of an engine that spells danger, watching for any kind of light in the murk.

Where are the trawlers now? Ten minutes ago, I nearly ran into one. I misread his lights, found myself dangerously close and on a collision course, and we both had to take simultaneous avoiding action.

I am tired. Last night was all sail changes. Tonight, I badly need a good long rest. By tomorrow evening, I should be coming on soundings on the Nantucket Shoals. Between now and then, I have a major shipping lane to cross, and some tricky navigating to do.

Where are those trawlers? I try calling them up on the Seavoice VHF set. But they do not listen to VHF. I turn on my foghorn, which is timed to go off once every two minutes. When I bought it in Southampton in April, it shook every shelf in the shop. Now its noise is nothing more than a baleful bleat, quickly lost in the surrounding gloom.

I feel cold. I go below to make some soup, and find everything is already damp. But the soup helps a bit. I put on another two sweaters, a pair of gloves and my polar-suit long-johns. It is the first time since Plymouth that I have needed to wear the long-johns. The hurricane lamp in the backstay starts to flicker. In about half an hour it will go out unless I go and play with it; eventually, I shall have to take it down and clean it. The hurricane lamp has been one of the major disasters of the trip. When it burns, it is as bright as any buoy on the ocean, casting a brilliant white light all around, and acting at once as a signal to other ships that I am there and as my decklight. But the paraffin I bought for it at a petrol station in Plymouth is not pure enough. After two hours, carbon starts to build up on its plunger, after three hours it is dead. All across the Atlantic, every night, I have had to tear myself out of sleep to keep that light going.

Tonight, I know I am not going to sleep again, and I am quite glad of an excuse for something to do. I go through a

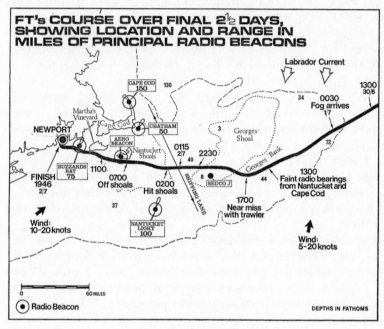

FT's COURSE OVER FINAL 2½ DAYS, SHOWING LOCATION AND RANGE IN MILES OF PRINCIPAL RADIO BEACONS

2 *FT*'s course over final 2½ days.

routine that I must have done a hundred times during the previous 26 days at sea. Put on both harness lines; attach the long harness line to the aft end of the cockpit; climb onto *FT*'s counter, the aft-most point of the deck; attach the short harness line to the backstay; with one arm round the backstay, release the spring clip and lift the hurricane lamp out of its holder; then slowly, gingerly, make my way back to the safety of the cockpit, trying not to lose balance or knock the lamp on the way.

Tonight, I stay for some time standing on the counter, with the sea rushing past me at $7\frac{1}{2}$ knots, just two feet below where I am standing. As I stand there, on the very stern of the boat, I am suddenly jolted into a realisation of the position I am in. Peering ahead, I can only just make out the bow, 35 feet ahead of me. Alone at night, you are aware of the fog, but you cannot see it. But now I know the worst. Visibility is about 20 yards. At the speed I am travelling, I shall have no time to avoid another ship, even if I see her at the last moment. I go back to the cockpit and sit down to make an appraisal of my position. I am on the edge of the Georges Bank, one of the busiest fishing grounds on the Atlantic coast, and I am going to be crossing it for most of the next twenty-four hours. The major danger, therefore, is trawlers rather than ocean-going shipping. What are the chances of a trawler either seeing or hearing me? The more I think about it, the more the chances seem to be pathetically low. During those long winter months before setting out on this race, I had carefully gone through all the dangers, and had tried to minimise them. For the past three and a half weeks I have been crossing three thousand miles of ocean, confident that if another ship was on a collision course with me, there was an overwhelming chance that he would see me. Now, I realise that the odds—and singlehanded sailing is all about odds—are for the first time against me. One by one, I mentally tick off my safety apparatus, and one by one, I find it to be wanting.

Lights: I have two sets of lights. At the top of the mast, about fifty feet above the water, are my red, green and white navigation lights. In the backstay is the hurricane lamp. It is just possible, I tell myself, that the fog at masthead level is thinner than at deck level, and that my navigation lights will be visible at some distance off. Alternatively, the very powerful hurricane light just might be throwing out a milky glow through the fog that another ship will see before she is on top of me. But these are remote chances. For all practical purposes, my lights are useless.

Radar: My radar reflector is at the top of the mast, to give maximum range. On the way across, I have several times checked with other ships to whom I have been talking on the radio whether they can see me on their radar screens. I know, therefore, that the reflector is well angled, that it sends back quite a sharp signal, and that its signal is quite distinct at a range of eight miles. But that was in mid-ocean, where ships are supposed to run regular watches. Fishermen in general and trawlers in particular are notoriously careless of other shipping. They talk to each other on their own trawler radio band (which I do not have) but do not listen to VHF (which I do). Once they have located each other, they get on with their fishing, and small boats, particularly small sailing boats, are expected to look after themselves. The chances of a fisherman keeping an eye on his radar screen, even in this weather, are remote.

Noise: I knew before I started that I was likely to meet fog near the American coast. Warm air flows off the hot American land mass at this time of year onto the cold Labrador Current that runs southwards from Newfoundland to New York, and creates classic conditions for what is known as advection fog. That was why I bought the foghorn and went to great lengths to fit it with a timing device so that I could leave it on and go to sleep. Now I am using it for the first time in earnest, and it just is not powerful enough. I guess that its whining hoot is not travelling more than fifty yards—a hundred yards at the outside. It is so weak that a trawler would be most unlikely to hear it over its engines. I leave it on—I leave it on for the whole of the next twenty-four hours. It is no more than a gesture.

Far more likely than that the enemy will hear me is that I shall hear them, either their engines or their own foghorn. That is why I decide I cannot afford to risk sleep. Again, the chances that I will hear anything, or that I shall see another ship in time to detach the self-steering and take avoiding action, are slim. But to stay awake seems slightly to reduce the odds, even if it does raise a whole host of different dangers associated with fatigue—falling overboard, making a navigational error, reacting too slowly to the needs of the boat.

As the night wears on, I long for dawn. Dawn will bring warmth, I shall be able to *see* the fog, perhaps it will not be as bad as I think it is. But when dawn arrives, it does not help. The fog is just as thick as I had feared, the boat remains damp. There is just one compensating factor. The sea is very flat, and the wind is light but steady—just the weather that *FT* likes best.

She is under maximum sail, with her huge overlapping genoa and full main, steaming along at just under 8 knots and bang on course.

When the sun comes up, I can see that the fog is a shallow one—its ceiling just two or three hundred feet above sea level, offering me occasional tantalising glimpses of blue sky. But it never leaves me all day. From time to time it lifts to give me half a mile or even a mile of visibility, and once I even see the white shape of the sun peering at me through it all. Hope springs eternal in these circumstances, and I dart below and fetch up the sextant to try and take a sight. But by the time I have invented a horizon, and start to make allowances for the refraction of light through the fog, I have forgotten the minute at which I took the sight, and by the time I go back on deck, the sun has gone again. The whole exercise is in practice a waste of time. I am now about a hundred miles from the Nantucket Shoals, and I need to know *exactly* where I am—for which I need a proper horizon and a clear sun. But it is something to do; something to relieve the monotony of sitting in the cockpit, looking and listening into the fog, trying to stay warm and awake. It is now the middle of Thursday, July 1, and the last decent sleep I had was on Monday night. Some twelve hours ahead of me is the Nantucket shipping lane and my 'Shoalfall'.

My reaction to all that is happening to me on this Thursday is largely fatalistic. Sailing has always been for me an experience in which I feel at one with my surroundings. Back in London, I live an extremely active life. I work too hard and burn up too much energy for my own good. But whenever life seems to be in danger of getting on top of me, I have a way out. I go to sea. All I need to do is get in a boat and set sail, and within hours, the whole land-based load will have left me. The sea has never yet let me down. For this reason, I suppose, I have never been frightened by it. I have been wet and cold and miserable and often seasick. I have longed for a storm to go away or a leak to stop dripping or for a particularly arduous voyage to end. But white-faced fear or panic—never.

So on this Thursday, fear has no place in a whole jumble of emotions. To start with, I have a lot to be pleased about. After 26 days at sea, I am 150 miles from the finish of a venture that began as an impossible dream four years ago, a pure fantasy which fortune and fate have allowed me to live out. If this wind holds, I am going to arrive in 27 days—a day shorter than the target I had set myself. I may well win the *Jester* Trophy for the small class in the race. That was what I set out to do four years ago. I had no idea then that there would be 82 starters for the *Jester* Trophy, or that it would provide the only real competitive racing in this year's *Observer* Singlehanded Transatlantic Race (OSTAR).

I am beginning to anticipate the finish. I am going to see my wife, hear news of my 15-month-old son (our first). I am soon going to be out of danger; and the worry, the pangs of guilt at the irresponsibility of a newly-married man with a small child setting out on a venture like this, will be past. I shall *know* at last how well or badly I have done—I have not seen another sailing boat since the Scilly Isles. Swapping stories over the yacht club bar; champagne and lobster at one of Newport's famous restaurants; a long night's uninterrupted sleep; phone calls to England; articles I must write when I land; the holiday that Elizabeth and I have planned when I arrive—all these suddenly seem so close.

Then there is the joy of being at sea. *FT* is putting on a command performance today. She is averaging very nearly 8 knots, her biggest sails are up and drawing, she is close hauled and dead on course for the shoals, steering just south of due west. I know *FT* now better than I shall know another boat again. I feel her every need. I listen to all her little noises, answer her every whim. The happy gurgle of the water running past the hulls sounds more excited than at any time during the race. The Atlantic ocean and its huge swells are behind us now, and we are back in coastal water, and the gentle ripples on the surface of the Georges Bank feel just like the Solent when it is fluffed by a breeze. I am constantly playing with the boat, sniffing the wind, glancing at the instruments, looking over the sails, checking the compass course, letting out an inch on a sheet here, taking in half an inch on a winch there.

When I was learning to sail as a small boy, my father used to come into my room just before I went to sleep to talk to me about sailing and winning races. 'You reach a point', he used to say, 'when you are no longer sailing the boat, but you become married to her. You and she fuse into one, and you feel her needs as if they were your own.' *FT* and I have been alone together for 26 days, and the bond between us is very close.

A blend of all these feelings helps sustain me through the dangers of this Thursday. Danger at sea is a passing phenomenon that those who love the sea learn to live with, knowing that when it is past it will be quickly forgotten. *FT* and I have had some bad moments on this trip, and before this Thursday is out, we shall go through the worst moments of our life together. You come to know that nothing lasts forever, that fog ultimately lifts, storms eventually abate, seas at some point calm down. While in them, you do all you can to stay alive, to minimise the dangers and, for the rest, you have to rely on luck.

Today, I feel exhaustion creeping in on me and that worries me; I have to spend a lot of time in the cabin below, navigating or cooking. Navigation is critical today—I *must* know where I am, and the one instrument that should be helping me to find out—my echo-sounder—is as usual working on feet but not on fathoms. Since I am in something between 17 and 20 fathoms of water, the feet dial is not much use to me and is proving wildly inconsistent.

While I am below, which is between a quarter and a third of the time, I can hear very little, and I have consciously to look all round me to see if anything is there. At the speed I am travelling, with 40 yards' visibility, these occasional scans of the horizon are quite inadequate as a lookout. So I am relying for much of the time on two things—on the other man keeping better watch than me, and on the odds against my being on a collision course with someone else. Meanwhile, I struggle to stay awake. Among other things, I tell myself, I shall have a better chance of surviving if I collide when awake than when asleep. I keep the boat going as fast as possible—I have a race to win. I have taken all the precautions I know how to, and for the rest, I shrug off the danger and wait for it to pass.

In one sense, I discover later in Newport, I am lucky. Many competitors who had taken a more northerly route than I were in this thick fog for a week. Mike Birch in *Third Turtle* simply ignored it, and kept sailing and sleeping as if it were not there.

Clare Francis in *Robertson's Golly* found herself in thick fog and surrounded by icebergs. At one point, the fog lifted and she looked behind her, and found her boat had just sailed a course straight between two bergs. In the previous race, Bill Howell in *Tahiti Bill* ran straight into the side of a Russian trawler at 8 knots in conditions very similar to those in which I find myself on this Thursday. The damage he sustained forced him to retire. If he had been 40 yards further back on his course, he would have run into the Russian's trawl wires, and he and his boat might have been dragged under water by the nets.

The fog near the finish of the OSTAR is the most dangerous part of the race. I spoke to the skipper of a fully crewed sailing boat who came through the fog four days after me. On every watch, he had one man stationed on the bow looking forwards, another man in the cockpit looking aft with his finger permanently on the motor starter button, another man steering and another navigating. The other watch looked after the sail changes. That is the seamanlike way to sail across fishing banks in fog. Alone, you can only minimise the risks. There is no way you can pretend you are being seamanlike.

As Thursday morning wears on, the wind gradually freshens, and I change down to the no. 2 genoa, and then take some reefs into the main. The wind is a steady force four now, but the sea remains no more than a popple, and *FT* continues to forge through it. At 1300 GMT (about 9 a.m. local time) comes a moment that I have waited for with increasingly eager anticipation. I plot my dead reckoning position on the chart and find I am almost within range of both the Nantucket light vessel and the Cape Cod Radio beacons. I fix up my Brookes and Gatehouse radio direction-finding (RDF) equipment, fit the earphones onto my head, and tune into the frequencies of the two beacons. There, faint but distinct, are the signals. Slowly, I point the RDF receiver in the direction of the signal. As I do so, the signal becomes fainter and fainter, and then dies entirely. This is the 'null point', which tells me where the signal is coming from. Having found it, all I need to do is to take a compass bearing, and I know roughly where I am in relation to that radio beacon. With two radio beacons, I can take cross bearings, and where the lines cross is where I should be.

I am about 140 miles from the Cape Cod beacon, and about 100 from the Nantucket light. The signals I receive are faint and imprecise. But they are music in my ears. Those radio beacons represent the end of the trip. I now know approximately where I am—it turns out to be some 15 miles south of my dead reckoning position, which means I am getting some south-going Labrador Current pushing me in the direction I want to go. Half an hour later, I do the same again, and then half an hour later once more. The positions I am plotting are forming a neat straight line on the chart, just where they should be. Gradually, my confidence builds up that I know my position. If only the depth meter would work. The chart says I am now in 18 fathoms of water. When I turn on the echo sounder, it just points at 12 fathoms every time.

At 1700 GMT, I am bent over my chart table, pencil in one hand, dividers in the other, trying to concentrate through my tiredness, trying not to make a mistake. There is a blaring siren. It rises and falls in tone like those on American police cars. I look up through the cabin window, and see, 30 yards away from me, a trawler coming out of the fog, his helm hard a-port, the whole boat lurching to starboard, a man in the wheelhouse staring furiously at me. All this I register in a split second. I am already on deck, leaning into the aft cockpit, jolting the self-steering out of place so that I can steer *FT* myself. But the danger is past, the trawler is going to miss me. I stand up in the cockpit and find myself waving to him. It is the first human face I have seen for 26 days. He just stares back. I notice his radar scanner is working, that he is not trawling but just chugging out towards his fishing grounds, travelling at about 15 knots. He had been on a course at exact right angles to mine. If he had not seen me in time, he would have hit me broadside on and amidships.

Within seconds, he has gone. I stare after him, trying to comprehend what has happened. My legs are shaking, and I find myself looking idiotically into the fog from the direction that he came. I dart below, switch on the VHF and try to call him up. But of course he is not listening. I go back on deck, sit on the edge of the cockpit, and try and calm down. Slowly, everything goes back to normal again. Gradually, I make myself believe that that was my near miss, and I won't have another one. I go down below, take off my oilskin jacket, and put on a lifejacket underneath it.

Later in Newport I hear some of the other stories of the fog. Alain Gabbay in the monohull *Objectif Sud III* heard a loud report while he was cooking. He arrived on deck in time to see the trawling arm of a passing boat miss his backstay by inches. Next morning, he discovered what the noise had been—the trawler's arm had hooked his topping lift and it had parted. A few inches closer and he would have lost his mast; a few feet and he would have had a head-on collision.

Another competitor found himself drifting helplessly in the fog when he heard an engine nearby. He sounded a signal on his foghorn to indicate he was unable to manoeuvre. The trawler sent him the same signal back—he was fishing and could not move. For 15 minutes, he waited for the trawler to loom out of the fog and crunch him to pieces.

The next few hours pass faster than any others on the trip. I am going to have to come on soundings without seeing a thing, that is clear. Besides the fishing vessels, there is one major navigational danger I have to avoid. We were warned in Plymouth that an oil drilling rig with the thoroughly unalluring name of *Sedco J* is drilling on the southern edge of the Georges Bank, and that it is held in place by a series of buoys with one mile hawsers. I have decided to give it a berth of at least five miles, but at present my course is taking me straight at it. I ease my sheets to pass to the north of it.

I check through all my charts, making sure they are in the right order. I take one and carefully plot on it a series of straight lines from the Nantucket light vessel across the shoals. I draw six lines, each 10 degrees apart, each representing a magnetic bearing onto the light vessel, and mark them accordingly. That way, if I take a quick RDF reading and find, for instance, that it is bearing 185 degrees, then all I need to do is glance at the chart and I know that I am half-way between the 180-degree line and the 190-degree line. I do the same thing for the aero beacon on the western end of Nantucket Island. Now I have a series of lines crossing each other, each representing bearings on the two radio beacons. With those two beacons to guide me, I should not have too much trouble when the time comes. By doing all this plotting in advance, I should minimise the danger of error through fatigue or through rushing things. It is going to be vital to know exactly where I am as I cross the shoals. The charts show depths of as little as 8 feet, and include all kinds of ominous looking notes—'breakers', 'race water'. The trouble with radio beacons is that you can only hear them for one minute in every six. If for some reason you miss them, or you fluff the bearing, you must wait another six minutes before the signal comes on again.

Then there are the tides, which run through the shoals at up to 2½ knots. I look them all up and write the information down—exactly when the tide will be running north, and when south, and at roughly what speeds. The information is stuck just above the chart table.

Then a good meal. All the way across, I have eaten well. I had read after the last race how the 1972 winner, Alain Colas, had stocked up on the best French pâtés and tinned food. I decided that food should be an important morale booster on my way across. Besides, I had learned on previous long sails that I suffer serious weight loss while at sea—in the 1974 Round Britain Race I lost 21 lbs.

In April before the OSTAR, I sailed over to Cherbourg at Easter and invaded the shops with Elizabeth. Tins of Poulet Chasseur, Canard à l'Orange, Rognons Sautés, Fricandeau de Riz, Pâté de Foie and Terrine de Chevreuil were piled into *FT* and taken home. Back in London, I went round to Robert Jackson in Knightsbridge—more pâté, lobster bisque and Cornish prawn soup. All that plus enough chocolate to feed an army, plenty of fresh fruit and all the usual staples meant I was never hungry and that I always looked forward to meals.

Today, I am both tired and hungry, and I have a long night ahead. I heat up some soup (I have a little two-burner gas stove with a grill), open a can of Canard à l'Orange and place it on the other burner. Then, while I am eating the soup, I use the soup saucepan first to boil up some freeze-dried 'Surprise' peas, then to mix a dollop of 'Smash' instant mashed potatoes. I take the main course back on deck, sit on the edge of the cockpit, have a quick check round the boat to see that everything is as it should be, make a couple of fine adjustments to the sheets and the self-steering, and then settle down to eat it. The orange sauce is delicious; the canard was indubitably once part of a duck and there is more of it than I can eat; the potato and peas, with a nob of margarine over both, and gently sprinkled with salt, mop up the sauce; then it is chocolate and a cup of coffee to round off the meal. While eating it, I keep my eyes and ears straining into the fog. Every time I come on deck now, I feel relieved that I am going to be keeping a proper lookout again; every time I go below to the relative warmth of the cabin, I persuade myself that whatever I have to do there is more important than keeping watch.

It is now 2230 GMT, about 6.30 p.m. local time. I am off the Georges Bank, sheets eased slightly to the south-south-westerly wind, creaming along at over 8 knots. The signals from the Nantucket light vessel are crystal clear, the null point quite distinct. I now have three radio beacons within range—Nantucket, Chatham and Cape Cod, and the bearings are crossing each other at almost exactly the same spot. I turn on the Seavoice VHF set and call up any shipping that can hear me on Channel 16. It is the fifth time today that I have done it, but this time I get a cheerful reply. 'This is yacht Foxtrot Tango, yacht Foxtrot Tango, does anyone receive me, does anyone receive me?' Crackle, crackle, somebody is switching on their transmitter. 'Foxtrot Tango, this is the *Fred H. Moore*, oil survey ship from Texas. I receive you loud and clear over.' We chat away for ten minutes. He is in the middle of the shipping lane, but about 10 miles to the north of me. Visibility, he warns me, is zero, and there is no let-up in the fog forecast. There is no escape. I must cross one of the busiest shipping lanes in the world blindfold. He has never heard of the Singlehanded Trans-atlantic Race, and is frankly stunned at what I am doing. Can he communicate with the land, I ask him. Why yes, he's from Texas, isn't he? I give him the telephone number of race head-quarters at Newport. Can he please ring them, tell them that I shall finish tomorrow, and to contact my wife? And can he please find out for me how many boats have finished, and whether anyone from the *Jester* class has arrived yet. Why sure, he can do that (the accent is a beautiful Texas drawl). 'Stand by on Channel 16, and I'll call you back in fifteen minutes.'

Fifteen minutes go by—no call. Then after half an hour I hear my call sign coming over the radio. 'Yacht Foxtrot Tango, yacht Foxtrot Tango, this is the *Fred H. Moore* here, this is the *Fred H. Moore* here, do you receive me? over.' I try and answer him. No response. He comes on again, but this time I only just hear him. He is right at the limit of my radio's range. We cannot talk to each other. Ten minutes later, I find myself talking to another ship. The radio officers are invariably friendly. 'A sailing boat, eh? Singlehanded from England. A race did you say? Well golly gee!' We had been told before the start that coastal shipping would be warned of our arrival. Not a single ship I talk to today has ever heard of the race. I explain to this one my truncated conversation with the *Fred H. Moore*. Would he mind contacting the *Fred H. Moore* and relaying the answer to me. Five minutes later he comes back. The *Fred H. Moore*'s message is: 'There are five arrivals at Newport. Good luck.'

Five arrivals in Newport. My head spins with this information. Eight days ago, when I had a thousand miles to run, I had heard on the BBC that Clare Francis in *Robertson's Golly* was also a thousand miles from the finish. I did not regard Clare as the principal competitor in the small boat *Jester* class, and the news that she and I were level pegging meant that I was doing badly. It also spurred the male chauvinist pig in me to greater efforts. Every pretence I ever had to being a liberated male was dashed at the prospect of being beaten in the singlehanded transatlantic race by a 5-foot 2-inch girl, and a very pretty one at that. Sorry, Germaine and Betty. I have failed the ultimate test. I just could not and would not be beaten by Clare.

That little burst of self-knowledge had come eight days ago. Then on Tuesday, two days ago, I had a long radio chat with the skipper of a passing German ship, the *New England Trapper*, who was as excited to meet me in mid-ocean as I was to meet him. He told me for the first time of the early disasters in the race—how *Kriter* had sunk and *ITT* been abandoned; how *Club Méditerranée* had put into St John's; how Tabarly appeared to be lost, after a series of false radio reports, one of which I had heard. But most importantly of all, Captain Manske of the *New England Trapper* told me that at that moment there were no finishers; (he turned out subsequently to be about seven hours out of date. Tabarly had finished that morning).

I was stunned by this news. At the time I was 450 miles from the finish. Apart from Clare Francis, I had no idea where anyone was. I thought I had done so badly during the first ten days that I had given up all hope of winning. But during those early days in the race, the boats to the north of me must have encountered some terrible storms, which I had missed altogether. Supposing—just supposing . . . perhaps I was going to win the *Jester* Trophy; perhaps even the whole race. But no, that was impossible. One of the big boats *must* arrive in under 25 days, and the best I could hope for was 27. But what of my *Jester* rivals? There was Clare to the north of me—surely one of the French monohulls would be ahead of her. Then there were the three tiny Newick-designed Val trimarans. One of them had been just behind me at the Scillies. Wouldn't they have been hit even more badly by the persistent strong south-westerly headwinds of the first ten days? I would beat the much lighter Val trimarans, I decided. But one of the heavy *Jester* monohulls would get there first.

Now I have this tantalisingly incomplete information. There are five boats at Newport; and I am 100 miles from the finish. Who are they? And are any of them *Jester* class boats? I must be winning my class—after all, I am over a day ahead of my target time. I can't be winning—I lost too much time at the beginning, I made a terrible mistake in the second week, one of the small boats will have got through without any mistakes at all. Tomorrow, I shall know. Whatever happens now, I am going to do well, the effort will have been worth it, I can *really* enjoy that meal in Newport when I get there.

Thus do I approach the shipping lanes and the shoals, tired, exhilarated, nearer exhaustion than I know, feeding off nervous energy, aware that the greatest danger of the whole trip still lies ahead of me.

At 0115 GMT, 9.15 p.m. local time, I take a bearing on the Nantucket radio beacon. I am right on the edge of the Nantucket separation zone, where all the coastal traffic is converging, where shipping is strictly enjoined to stay in lane and to stay on course. I have to cut straight across it. I put a call out on the radio to any shipping. No answer. I go on deck,

peer into the gloom to port. I can hear nothing, I can see no
more than 30 yards. I just stay on deck, glued to the cockpit,
praying that no ships would dare come into this shipping lane
in this kind of weather without radar. My foghorn bleats uselessly every two minutes—perhaps a ship with a watch stationed

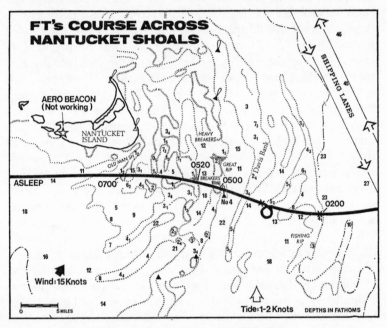

3 *FT*'s course across the Nantucket shoals.
I shall never know precisely where I went in the early hours of
July 2. This is my best guess. The two Xs are taken off the chart
I was using at the time. One chilling discovery I made in
writing this book—the tide was running northwards. In the state
of near-exhaustion I was in at the time, I convinced myself that
it was carrying me away from Nantucket Island towards safety.

right up on the bow may hear it. *FT* holds steady on a course
of 280 degrees magnetic, just south of west, where she has been
for hours, her sheets eased a little, moving at over 8 knots.

I go down below and put yet another general call out on the
radio on Channel 16. At last I get an answer. I am in a high
state of nerves, and the radio officer picks up the tension. Yes,

he is looking at his radar screen, and there is nothing near him, I need have no worry. I tell him my course—straight across his shipping lane. 'Just keep going as you are,' he intones. 'You'll be all right. No one would use this shipping lane tonight without radar.' Can he see me on his radar screen? There is one yacht that he can see, and he gives me its position. That can't be me—it's too far west. His position would place me on the far side of the shipping lane, and I know I am roughly in the middle of it. The conversation is cut short by my need to take a bearing on the Nantucket light. I get the bearing and plot it on the chart—198 degrees more or less. It is not as good a bearing as I would like. I look at the chart. I *am* already through the shipping lane. In fact, I must be *on* the Nantucket Shoals. I turn on the echo-sounder. It reads 20 feet. Almost literally, I have hit America. It is 0200 GMT, 10.00 p.m. local time.

I switch the echo-sounder from feet to fathoms. At 20 feet it should read $3\frac{1}{2}$ fathoms. As usual, it reads 12. It has never worked properly since it was installed. Now I must find exactly where I am. The Nantucket Shoals are notoriously dangerous, I have only had radio by which to navigate all day, I could easily be five or ten miles further north or south than I think.

I tune into the frequency of the aero beacon on the west end of Nantucket Island. With that and Nantucket to guide me, I should soon know to within a mile or two where I am. I play with the Brookes and Gatehouse dials, turn the volume up, adjust the headset, double check that I have all the dials set right. It is no good. The aero beacon is not working. All I have got is Nantucket.

Never mind. I shall take some running fixes off Nantucket. If I take one now, and one in six minutes' time, and provided they are both precise bearings, then I can draw two lines on the chart. I know my course, and I shall know from the log how far I have gone in those six minutes. All I shall then need to do is lay my course and the distance run across the two lines, and I shall know exactly where I am.

I look at my watch. Time to catch the Nantucket light signal. I go on deck with the radio direction finder, and try to get an accurate reading. The signal is there all right, but the null point is no longer distinct. The last bearing I took was reasonably precise. Now, there is a range of 10 degrees within which the null point could lie. I make a wild guess, go down below and write it down. But even as I do so, I know it is not good enough. To take a running fix, you need to be really accurate. What has happened to the Nantucket radio beacon? With a start, I see the problem. While I have been crossing the shipping lane, night has fallen. Of course. In how many books have I read that at dusk, RDF loses its precision. From now on, the radio beacon will serve as no more than a rough guide. What I need to know is *precisely* where I am.

My situation is extremely serious. The only thing I know for certain is that I have been in water that is 20 feet deep. Allowing a margin of error to the echo-sounder, that is something between three and $4\frac{1}{2}$ fathoms. The chart shows three places where the most easterly of the Nantucket Shoals is down to 4 fathoms. I could be in any of these three places. I mark an X on the chart where I think I am—on a shoal called the Fishing Rip. I could be ten miles further north—in which case, my present course will take me straight into Nantucket Island; or I could be ten miles further south, in which case there are two unlit buoys in my path which I have not a hope of seeing. The aero beacon is definitely not working—four or five times I try to find it, and four or five times there is only silence. Nantucket beacon is giving me a very rough guide as to where I am—but only very rough.

With the coming of night, fatigue and exhaustion are beginning to cripple my mind. I have to fight the temptation to just go on deck and sail on through the night and the fog. Stay awake, don't lose it. I am talking to myself, at times shouting at myself to keep my mind in order. Once before, I have experienced total exhaustion alone at sea. That time, my brain played havoc with me, and filled my mind with illusory objects. Talk to yourself, tell yourself what you're doing, argue every decision through out loud. Concentrate on finding our where you are.

Someone, somewhere is looking after me tonight. The echo-sounder is now reading 40 feet—about 7 fathoms. Feeling helpless, I switch over to fathoms, knowing full well that the needle will point desultorily at 12. But it does not. It points to seven. For the first time in three seasons, it is working. Providence has intervened.

This is a vital gain. In a few minutes, I should be in 14 or 15 fathoms of water—off the end of the foot dial. But with the echo-sounder now working on fathoms, I can quite literally watch the bottom as I sail over it. Every time there is a change I must write down my log reading and my course. Write it down. Don't forget.

I am now talking to myself all the time, trying to keep my thinking processes in order, trying not to make a mistake. Soon the dial should rise to about 14 fathoms. There she goes—9, 10, 14 fathoms. Take a log reading. Write it down.

Slow down, *FT*, slow down. I must find out where I am before you go any farther. I ease the jib sheet, let off a bit of main. Her speed slackens from over 8 knots to just under 8—still too fast. I try putting her into irons. But she just tacks herself, and it takes thirty debilitating minutes to get her straight again. Where have I been during that half hour? I don't know. But I cannot afford to waste energy like that again. Put her on course and leave her there. Just concentrate on finding where you are.

Take a log reading, write it down. What's the depth? Still 14 fathoms, we cannot have strayed all that far during all that messing about. You must find your position. Talk to yourself. Slowly, deliberately talk to yourself. It has worked before. It will work now. Don't let go of your consciousness. The boat is being looked after. I know that.

When I sail singlehanded, I talk to myself a lot, splitting myself into two people who argue things through together. Tonight, one mistake could cost me my life, the boat, the race, in that order. But I am not thinking in those terms; just to get across these shoals and off the other side without letting go. It is my third night running without sleep. Hold on. Keep talking to yourself. The boat is in good hands.

There is the Nantucket call sign. Try and get a reading. It is somewhere between 180 and 190, probably about 187. The echo-sounder reads 16 fathoms. I mark an X on the chart where I think I am. If I am right, then in half an hour, after another four miles' sailing, I should hit a 4-fathom shoal. By the time

I have worked this out, checked and double checked it, the half hour has almost gone. Right on cue, the echo-sounder starts to fall: 9, 8, 6, 4 fathoms; and there it hovers for two miles.

This must be the Davis Bank. It could not be anything else. But where am I on it? I could still be farther north than I think. I could still be heading straight for Nantucket Island. Or I could be at the latitude of red buoy no. 4, which would be $2\frac{1}{2}$ miles away.

Red buoy no. 4. I must not hit that. It has a flashing light on it. I just might see it—then I would know where I am. Go back on deck and keep watch for it. On deck there is fog and darkness all around me. When was I last on deck? Thirty or forty minutes ago. Who has been watching for fishing boats? No one. Who has been listening for any breakers on the shoals? No one. Who has been checking the wind strength, adjusting the sails? No one. Yet down below, I have been concentrating so hard on the problem in hand that I have mentally consigned all these other responsibilities to someone else who is not there.

I watch for twenty minutes but see nothing. Instead, precisely on cue, the fathom meter drops to almost zero. I switch over to feet. 10 feet. I am on the Great Rip Bank. Three minutes later, back into 6 fathoms. My confidence is beginning to build up. I have been on the shoals for three hours. The sea is calm, no sign of breakers. The wind is veering and heading me a little, but it is continuing to blow at the same steady 15–18 knots that it has blown all day. What am I doing in weather like this on a lee shore? If I had tried to sail round the shoals, I would have lost two or three precious hours. I am back on deck, adjusting my sheets to the change of wind. I can just hold a course of 280 degrees M., a little south of due west.

Twenty minutes later, we hit the next shoal. Another two hours' sailing and we are finally clear, in 14 fathoms of water.

It is now 0700 GMT, 3 a.m. local time. I have been on the shoals for five hours. Throughout that time, I have heard nothing and seen nothing. There are no shoals ahead, and therefore probably no fishing boats. I am too close to land to be in the path of coasters. I make myself a coffee and drink it. Two hours till dawn. Can I possibly stay awake for that time? I decide to try. After a few minutes, I find myself on the cockpit floor. I try standing up rather than sitting down. Even standing up, I begin to lose consciousness.

There are three things I can do. I can heave to—stop the boat entirely—and go to sleep; or I can put her on self-steering, take a nap and leave her on her present course which will steer her clear of all navigational obstacles; or I can try and stay awake. Heaving to is the safest—but then I will lose several hours, and possibly the race. I do not seriously consider that at all. Staying awake is probably impossible, and I am now so tired that even changing a sail would be dangerous. If I go to sleep and leave her steering herself, there is a minor chance of a collision. I decide that the dangers of collision are less than the dangers attendant on exhaustion. I fit on the battery-operated self-steering, which automatically steers a compass course. I set two alarm clocks to go off in three hours at 0900 GMT (5 a.m. local time), and collapse onto my bunk.

I sleep through both alarm clocks—one of them a repeater that goes off nine times, and both of them placed within inches of my head. I wake to find that I have overslept by nearly two hours. I try to get out of my sleeping bag and find I cannot—the whole of my right leg is cramped, and will not move in any direction. Slowly, and in some pain, I heave myself out of the sleeping bag and off the bunk with my arms. After some minutes I feel my leg moving again. While I have slept, the wind has veered from south-west to west-south-west, putting the boat about and leaving her hove to. It is broad daylight, but the fog is still down, though visibility seems to be better than I have grown used to—about $\frac{1}{4}$-mile. I look at the log—it reads 679. I have travelled about 20 miles through the water while asleep. That represents three hours' sailing. I take a bearing on Buzzards Bay radio beacon, about 25 miles ahead of me, check the depth (19 fathoms) and make a rough estimate of my course from the end of the shoals. Everything points to one spot on the chart, ten miles south of Martha's Vineyard. I make a little X on the chart, and get *FT* sailing again.

An hour later, at 1300 GMT, the fog lifts. There, five miles to the south of me, exactly where it should be, looking beautifully green against the glistening blue sea and sky, is Martha's

1 Close-hauled on her first sail, March 1974. This famous
picture illustrates *F T*'s major weakness—pitching in a
short sea. (*Glyn Genin*)

2 The OSTAR. An hour after the start, and *FT* is under full sail at 7½ knots. (*Ashley Ashwood*)

3 The author being towed into Newport after his 27-day crossing. Note the hurricane lamp in the backstay. (*Chris Smith*)

Vineyard. It is my first sight of land since the Scillies. The finishing line is 35 miles away. It is precisely 27 days and one hour since the start of the race at Plymouth.

The rest of this Friday is pure magic. All the tension of the previous two days flows out of me. This is the sort of day that those who love sailing dream of, which wipes out memories of the others. I become totally carefree. Nothing seems to be important enough to spoil this day. Already, I have the first inkling that I am not going to win the *Jester* Trophy—there is no aeroplane overhead taking pictures for tomorrow's *Financial Times* as there certainly would be if I was first in my class. I find myself abandoning safety routines that I have drilled into myself for nearly a month—here I am shaking out rolls in my mainsail without any safety harness on. I try to discipline myself again, but today, I cannot take seriously the thought of danger.

As the morning warms up, Rhode Island Sound fills with sails, all heading towards Martha's Vineyard and Nantucket Sound for the July 4 bicentennial weekend. I am sitting in the cockpit, wind about 15 knots across the deck, big no. 1 genoa and full main drawing perfectly, *FT* skimming across the rippling waves close-hauled at just under 8 knots, when I hear the roar of a motor boat's engine. I look under the genoa and there just ahead of my lee float is a day fishing boat, engine at full throttle, trying to get out of my way. I had not seen him. I had not even looked under my sail for fifteen minutes. For so long have I had the ocean to myself that the possibility of collision, the need to keep a constant lookout, is no longer instinctive and automatic. The three men and their fishing boat pass me just six feet away from my lee float, staring at me as if I were insane. How can they know that I have just sailed from Plymouth?

The sound is now a mass of white sails. As they pass me, many wave, some shout congratulations, whole boatloads of sunbathers lift themselves from their reveries and start spontaneously to clap. I find myself clapping back, waving, shouting, thrilled at the human contact.

I have left my VHF radio on standby, so that I can listen to the boats chattering among themselves and with the Coast

Guard. In England, VHF is the exception rather than the rule. Here, every boat in the sound seems to have radio. There are joky messages between sailors, messages being passed on for wives. '*FT*, *FT*, do you hear me, *FT*?' My own boat's name is crackling across the airwaves. I dart below and pick up the microphone. 'This is *FT*, David Palmer speaking, who is calling me?' 'David, this is John Ketteringham here. I am in the white sloop 50 yards to leeward of you with her sails flapping.'John Ketteringham, captain of the Oxford University Sailing team in my second year, whom I have not seen for eleven years; he married Rodney Pattisson's sister and went to live in America, and here he is, 50 yards away, talking to me. We talk for five minutes, and then I ask him if he can contact race control at Newport and find out if any *Jester* class boats are in. It is fifteen minutes before he comes back again, fifteen minutes of waiting to know for certain whether I have won or lost. Then back comes the message—there are six boats at Newport, two of them *Jester* class.

I am going to be third. It takes me little more than a minute to absorb the disappointment. Nothing, absolutely nothing can be allowed to spoil this perfect day. I have just 10 miles to go, about an hour and a half's sailing, the wind is slowly piping up, the tops of the little waves are beginning to break, I am down to no. 2 genoa and a reefed main, close-hauled and making $7\frac{3}{4}$ knots. I detach the self-steering and for the first time since the Scilly Isles, take the helm myself.

This is the end of my marriage to *FT*. I shall never sail her again, for she is to be sold in Newport. She has done almost everything I ever asked of her; she has brought me across the world's most awesome ocean fast and safely. For the last ten miles, I take her wheel in two fingers of my left hand. Together, totally at one with each other, we storm across the finishing line. It is 27 days, 7 hours, 45 minutes and 55 seconds since the starting gun boomed across Plymouth Sound.

I let everything go—the sheets, the helm, myself. I find myself shaking the air with my hands, shrieking at the sky that *FT* and I have done it, we have completed the transatlantic race, we have come third in our class. Frank Page of *The Observer* is alongside with a BBC camera crew, blaring information at me.

Elizabeth is on her way from New York by train; a tow-boat is coming out to me; *Third Turtle* and *Spaniel* are the two *Jester* boats to finish ahead of me—*Third Turtle* is one of the little Val trimarans that I have always considered a rival, but I know nothing about *Spaniel*.

I meet the tow-boat half-way into the harbour. Down sails, throw a line. Everyone is waving, shouting congratulations. In through all the moored boats, past the Goat Island Marina. Hundreds of people are lined up, cheering and clapping. There in the middle of them is Jurek Martin, the *Financial Times* US editor, a bottle of champagne held aloft. A little speed boat appears from the marina, with a familiar face smiling and waving from it. Elizabeth boards, we are in each other's arms, crying and laughing all at once.

Tie up alongside. 'Congratulations on being the first British boat to finish.' That can't be right. Where is Mike McMullen and *Three Cheers*? What has happened to all the big boats? Who else is in? Tabarly, Colas, Mike Birch in *Third Turtle*, Kazimierz Jaworski in *Spaniel*, Tom Grossman in *Cap 33*, Jean-Claude Parisis in *Petrouchka*—three Frenchmen, a Canadian, a Pole and an American. I am the first of over forty British starters to arrive.

Jurek is on board with his champagne; a press conference on the dockside where every journalist seems to be French; a call from the BBC Today programme in London. 'Can you describe the culture shock you feel on returning to dry land?' No I cannot. There is no culture shock. The land is not even moving under my feet. I am not equal to telling the BBC man in his London office how I feel. At this moment, I am more relaxed, more sated by life, more totally together and at one with myself than I have ever been before.

2

THE DREAM

June 1972. A typically lazy weekend with my father down in Devon. More out of duty than will, I picked up *The Sunday Times* and found myself without much enthusiasm setting out on a long dispatch from mid-ocean by Murray Sayle. Murray was sailing a catamaran called *Lady of Fleet* in the fourth *Observer* singlehanded transatlantic race. He was in no sense a serious competitor. Two weeks earlier, on the day the fleet set out from Plymouth, Murray's and *The Sunday Times*'s attitude to the race had been perfectly encapsulated in their front page headline:

OUR MAN LAST IN SINGLEHANDED START

Twenty minutes later, I put down the newspaper. I was hooked. I had been reading about the sea, about what it felt like to be alone in the middle of it, to sail away from everyone and everything and head for America.

Over the next few weeks, I found myself reading more and more on the race. There was the saga of Francis Chichester and his rescue; the thrilling victory of Alain Colas in a trimaran called *Pen Duick IV* over a giant 128-foot French schooner called *Vendredi XIII*; more articles from Murray Sayle. In his final dispatch, he was dismasted and towed to Newport.

The dream that began to occupy my mind was of course impossible. I had never competed in an ocean race in my life. I had never sailed singlehanded in anything larger than a dinghy. The previous season, the summer of 1971, had been the first I had ever sailed offshore. I knew nothing about astro-navigation. I had only done one season of coastal navigation. I had no money. In November, I would be starting a new and intensely challenging job at *The Financial Times*, which would more than occupy my energies over the next two years. There was also Elizabeth to consider—I had only known her for eight months, but it was going rather well, and I did not want to jeopardise it. Forget it, I told myself. You have no money, no experience and no time.

But something had caught hold of me that would not let go. The dream of the singlehanded transatlantic race is an intensely powerful one, combining romance, escapism, danger; providing a challenge that appeals to every sense in a sailing man's make-up.

All my life, I have sailed. I was in a boat when I was four. I was given my first dinghy when I was ten. I entered my first race at Itchenor Sailing Club when I was eleven. By the age of fifteen I had given up all other summer sports to concentrate on dinghy racing. The following year, aged sixteen, I won my first open race (to this day, I remember every tactical move of that race). At one time, I dreamed of the Olympic Games. But at the age when I might have had a go at that, I spent two years hitchhiking round the world instead, and by the time I got back, it seemed more important to get stuck into a career.

In the summer of 1971, I was thirty-one, old enough to see forty on the horizon, young enough to laugh at it. It was my second season as part of a syndicate, sharing a 30-foot Iroquois catamaran. The move over to cruising had left me with mild regrets at abandoning dinghy racing. But as my work became more demanding, cruising and offshore sailing were beginning to feel like the relaxation I needed.

Across the horizon flickered the Atlantic race. Why not? I asked myself. Money—I could probably find a sponsor; other people had in the past. Navigation—I could learn to use a sextant. A boat—it must be a multihull, a combination of Alain Colas and the Iroquois had convinced me of that. Offshore experience—most of what I needed to know I had learned in dinghies, and years of dinghy racing would be a solid base on which to build. But the real attraction of the *Observer* Single-handed Transatlantic Race (OSTAR) was the challenge it presented, and the more I dwelt on it, the more I wanted to take it on. To set out on a major project four years in advance; to plan a boat, build it, prepare it and myself for the race; to win the singlehanded transatlantic race. This is the ultimate challenge for a yachtsman—to race alone across one of the world's great oceans, and to beat the ocean and all your competitors. I had to do it.

A plan began to form in my mind. I would find a sponsor and build a boat in time for the 1974 Round Britain Race. The Round Britain is a two-man race, not singlehanded, but it would prove a valuable testing ground both for the boat and for me. I must find someone to do it with me who had experience in all the areas where I was wanting—ocean racing, tuning of an offshore boat, choosing offshore gear and equipment. The 1975 season would be a major work-up year for the Atlantic Race. By 1976, the boat and I should both be ready.

In October, I took Elizabeth out to dinner and told her of my plans. We discussed the dangers of the race, the amount of time it would take up, the potential strains it would put on ourselves. It was almost a year since we had first met, and I was not prepared to do it without her support. Her main concern was whether I could combine all this sailing activity with my new job. Mine was at the number of unknowns I was taking on at once—how would I react to being alone for long periods, to being caught in a storm? Was I being honest with myself about the dangers involved, and would I want to run away from them when they were translated into a real boat, a real ocean, a real race? Supposing that the whole project was a terrible failure? Would I be able to face up to it?

Two days later, I was among a group lunching with the chairman and chief executive of *The Financial Times*, Lord Drogheda. I brought up the transatlantic race and sketched out what I wanted to do. Would *The Financial Times* ever consider sponsoring such an exercise. Drogheda's face broke into a typically sardonic smile. But a month later, I learned that he was talking about the project to friends of his. The dream of the transatlantic race is indeed a powerful one.

In November, my new job started. I found myself working fourteen and fifteen hours a day, in a high state of nervous tension. At precisely that moment, the builder doing my house, who was already months behindhand, announced his impending bankruptcy. For three weeks, the transatlantic race receded into the background.

There it would probably have stayed but for a chance meeting over dinner one night with Luke FitzHerbert just before Christmas. I outlined what I wanted to do. He told me that he too had dreamed for years of doing the Round Britain Race, and would do it with me. We had all had a lot to drink, it was 1.00 a.m., and I woke next morning to a 7.30 confrontation with the builder and quickly forgot the previous evening's conversation. Two weeks later, Luke rang me. Was I serious? Let's meet for lunch.

Lunches surrounded by piles of old yachting magazines; late-night drives out into the country to meet designers, where we would huddle round fires and talk about the Atlantic ocean. Designers have to be patient people, subject to constant visits from dreamers, usually late at nights or at weekends, from most of whom they never hear another word.

We soon narrowed out list of potential designers down to three—Derek Kelsall, who has made his name as a trimaran man; Rod Macalpine-Downie, a catamaran specialist; and Michael Pipe, who had had some startling success with a long, narrow, bulb-keeled monohull called *Slithy Tove*, which he had designed and built for the 1970 Round Britain Race.

From the outset, I favoured a trimaran. I had never in my life sailed one, but my two summers with the Iroquois cat had persuaded me that cats were quite unsuitable for singlehanded sailing—they give little or no warning when they are thinking of capsizing, and I could not imagine myself going to sleep and leaving one sailing. A tri, on the other hand, with most of her weight concentrated in her centre hull, seemed—in theory at least—to present a far safer alternative.

We quickly settled on Derek Kelsall to be designer and builder. We could not find Michael Pipe in any known reference book, so instead, I rang Jack Holt and asked him if he felt he could build a long, thin, bulb-keeled monohull which could outsail multihulls. He said he was sure he could not, and after that we stopped thinking about monohulls. We had a long lunch with Rod Macalpine-Downie, who tried to persuade us that catamarans were no less stable than tris. He failed. Kelsall I had first met in 1966, when he designed and built a revolutionary trimaran called *Toria* and walked away with the Round Britain Race. He had the priceless advantage of running his own yard. He would therefore both design and build the boat, and the time-honoured problem of making sure that both designer and builder understood what each wanted from the other and when would be solved at the outset.

By now, we had settled on a number of decisions of principle that were to shape the boat that ultimately became *FT*. First, I would enter the small class for the transatlantic race—for boats with a waterline of less than 28 feet. I reasoned that I had a good chance of raising enough money for a small boat, none at all of raising several hundred thousand pounds for a large one. I also felt instinctively that the small class would provide the best racing and the biggest entry when the time came. In the event, 82 of the 125 competitors who crossed the starting line in June 1976 were entered for the *Jester* Trophy for small boats, and it turned out to be an extraordinarily competitive class.

Our next decision shaped everything else we did over the following months and years. Every piece of equipment that we bought must have had at least two full seasons' use. We would not buy anything experimental. This was the final reason for choosing Kelsall rather than Macalpine-Downie to design the trimaran—Kelsall had designed and built several, but for Macalpine-Downie this would have been his first. Under the heading 'too experimental', we also rejected the use of foils, water ballast in the outriggers, and any thought of playing around with a Proa design.

Into the spring of 1973, and a string of meetings with Kelsall; the first outline drawings which produced a thrill all of their own; budget estimates. By April, I was ready to put a formal proposal to *The Financial Times*. A month later came back the reply—'I am afraid the general feeling is that we would not be justified on promotional grounds . . .' Despair for several days, until Elizabeth calmed me down and persuaded me not to take no for an answer. More meetings with senior *Financial Times* executives; a phone call to Liz Balcon at *The Observer* publicity office to see if she had copies of the cuttings from the last race; a final presentation, armed with two sheaves of press cuttings. On June 26, 1973, three years to the day before my worst storm in the transatlantic race, *The Financial Times* board met and the project was on.

I quickly began gathering together a design team: Kelsall; Terry Pearce from International Yacht Equipment, who would design and build the spars; Peter Dove of Hood Sailmakers; and Ralph Farrant, skipper of *Trifle*, the most successful trimaran then racing. Furtively, we all met at the Royal Corinthian during Cowes week and started taking decisions. The mast would be deck-stepped and would not swivel—Terry Pearce said he could not promise that a swivelling mast would stay up under the extreme conditions presented by a flexing trimaran; reefing would be through mast roller; the mast would have steps attached to it, so that I could climb it in mid-Atlantic; the mainsail would be attached to mast and boom by bolt-rope. For four hours, we sat there talking and arguing, taking point by point. Kelsall, Dove and Pearce discussed the rig, mast and sail-plan, and modified their ideas according to each other's needs. Luke and I had come to the meeting with a particularly harebrained scheme to use only one winch. The logic was impeccable—if you are singlehanded, you can only use one winch at a time, so why have any more? In the end, we settled on a total of four winches in the cockpit, and one on the mast.

In October, 1973, we had our second and final design meeting at my house in London (Plate 8). It started at 8 p.m. and broke up in high spirits in the small hours of the morning, with a unanimous decision that *FT* would be uncapsizeable and unbeatable. The following day, work started on her at Derek Kelsall's yard at Sandwich.

There is a very special excitement about seeing a boat gradually emerge amid the debris of a boatyard. Every third weekend, I drove down to Sandwich to see how she was getting on. She was built in foam sandwich—a technique pioneered by Derek in which PVC foam is sandwiched between two layers of glass fibre to form a stiff but strong hull (Plates 4–7). At a very early stage, the outline of the main hull was clearly visible in the yard, and by December, there was the hull, the right way up, with one of the floats a-building alongside it.

But if these trips to Sandwich provided a sense of anticipation and thrill, in almost every other sense the winter of 1973–74 was a bad one. My job was gradually wearing me down to the point where I developed a painful and debilitating stomach illness, which a succession of doctors and a long line of not very pleasant tests failed to diagnose. (It turned out in the end to be a reaction to sustained stress.) In the middle of the winter, the Heath Government imposed a three-day week, and within days suppliers of vital raw material and equipment for *FT* began making excuses for late delivery. Back at *The Financial Times*, the Yom Kippur War fused with the oil crisis, which in turn led to a long winter of political and economic turmoil and ultimately to a General Election and the fall of the Heath Government. This is the raw material on which newspapers feed. In professional terms, it was among the most exciting periods I have lived through. But it was all taking a considerable physical and mental toll, and at Christmas, Elizabeth and I fled to Cumberland to try and recharge some batteries.

One result of all this was that I only managed to concentrate on *FT*'s problems in snatches. And it was in one of these snatches that I was asked by Derek Kelsall to approve a decision that was afterwards almost to prove the trimaran's undoing.

FT's beams had been shown on all the early drawings as round tubes made from extruded alloy sections, similar to standard metal masts. But in the course of the winter, it became clear that these sections were not available. One Saturday afternoon down at Sandwich, Derek showed me a drawing of beams using aluminium channel sections. Would I approve his using them? The whole discussion only lasted ten minutes, and I did not really think about it again. At that point in time, I knew nothing about multihull design, I have no qualifications in engineering, and I do not understand the properties of metals. I asked one or two questions about the relative strengths of the two beam designs, and gave the go-ahead. The one question I failed to ask was whether aluminium channel sections had ever been used in trimarans before. Had I done so, I would have learned that to use them would mean breaking our number one rule—no experiments.

The beams turned out to be the only hiccoughs in *FT*'s construction. In every other respect, her building proceeded without a hitch. Masts, spars, sails all turned up on time. Back in London, I slowly worked through a list of vital equipment that I had taken responsibility for ordering: winches from Gibb;

instruments from Baron; RDF from Brookes and Gatehouse. Each decision required many hours' wading through the advertisements in the yachting magazines, a series of telephone calls, comparisons of prices, of discounts offered and of what existing owners told me about the equipment. I was also spending two lunch hours every week at the City of London Polytechnic's School of Navigation, under the patient tutelage of Captain McLaren, learning the mysteries of declinations, azimuth angles, spherical triangles and intercepts. Down in Sandwich, Derek Kelsall and Emrys Barrell, his yard manager, performed miracles of scheduling to keep work on the boat going on in and around the three-day week.

At last came launch day. I had not been down to Sandwich for several weeks—the first of the two 1974 General Elections had been occupying me full-time. On a bitterly cold Saturday morning in early March, Elizabeth and I came round the bend in the road leading to the Sandwich marina, and there ahead of us, suspended in mid-air, was this pink trimaran, on her way to the water. It was my first sight of her in one piece. By the time we left Sandwich that evening (I had to work on the Sunday), her mast was up, and she was nestling gently against the edge of the river.

3

THE REALITY

March 17, 1974: A Sunday. For two days, a team of us has been trying to bring *FT* to the point where we can take her out of the Stour river, and over to Ramsgate harbour. The tide has been dropping now for an hour and a half. If we do not leave in ten minutes, we will never get across the sands at the entrance to the river. Forty minutes later, we are at least ready to go, the outboard starts first time, and we are heading down the river, past the Pfizer factory, and out to sea.

As we leave the river and start to cross the sands, it is clear we have left it too late. Even the middle of the channel here dries out to four feet at Low Water, and it is now just about half tide. On either side of the channel, which is only some twenty yards wide, the sea is already breaking over the sands, and a bitter north-easterly is blowing straight at us, making a nasty little chop. Soon we are in serious trouble. As *FT* starts to rise and fall to the waves, the outboard jumps in and out of the water. When the blade lifts out, the motor races fit to bust and the propeller thrashes uselessly at the air before plunging back into the water again. The centreboard grounds and we lift that right up; then we ground the rudder, and we lift that up too; then finally the main hull is stuck. We are on a lee shore, the wind shows every sign of increasing, in two hours' time it will be dark, and the tide is falling rapidly. I go and measure the depth off the starboard float—it is about nine inches. Luke goes and checks off the port float—it is two feet. We push and shove her to port, and get her to float again. Now we all stand on the stern to try and keep the motor in the water, while Emrys Barrell lies flat on his stomach, throttling back whenever the propeller starts to thrash thin air. For half an hour we move through the water like this, just managing to keep her moving forwards and to retain steerage way. At last, we see the Ramsgate pilot's boat ahead of us. She has come to tow us in, and is

44

waiting in the deep water while we negotiate the last hundred yards of the sands.

It could hardly have been a less auspicious beginning. For the first time, as I sat in the cockpit helplessly contemplating the possibility that *FT* might break up on the sands that night, I had realised the full size of the responsibility that I had taken on. Not only was *FT* not my boat; she was my employer's. For a brief and slightly panicky moment, I had wondered just where my job would be if *FT* came to an ignominious end before a sail had ever been hoisted.

March 23: *FT*'s first ever sail, and the day we have invited the press to come and photograph her. It is a grey day, but the boat makes up for that by proving herself to be a most photogenic lady. It is blowing force five, a moderately strong breeze, there is a sharp little sea running, and *FT* starts to buck in and out of the waves. It provides some superb pictures of her leaping out of the sea like a greyhound from a trap. On board, she is giving us all a thrilling ride, travelling at up to 8 knots on a close reach. But the very motion that is making her look so good on her pictures is causing one or two sidelong glances on board. A second or two after she jumps out of one wave, providing the photographers with their picture, she crashes into the next one. As she does so, the whole boat jars and shudders almost to a halt, the front edge of her forward cross beam thuds against the water, and she takes a second or two to pick up speed again. It is the first evidence we have of *FT*'s most enduring problem— her pitching in a sea. Her waterline is so short, and the expanse of boat and mast and sail sitting on top of it is so large, that once she starts to rock, the effect is rather like a pendulum with a heavy weight on the end. But on this maiden sail, we do not dwell too much on this. It is the first time in Luke's life that he has sailed a trimaran, and only my second. We put her through her paces, surge on and off waves, and all five of us on board take turns at the wheel. She is light and sensitive on the helm, and very responsive to the slightest touch; she has remarkable acceleration, responding almost instantly to adjustments in course or sail set; after two hours, we take her back to Ramsgate harbour, invigorated by the freezing cold wind and the excitement of the sail. At her mooring comes a shock. We lift the hatch covers on each of the floats, and find that both of them are about one-third full of water after just two hours' sailing.

Easter 1974: The first serious sail Luke and I do in *FT*. The two of us set out late on Maundy Thursday for the Schelde in Holland, where we spend two hard days testing the boat. It is mid-April, and most of the time the sun is out to relieve the cold. We quickly identify her strongest single point of sailing—going to windward in light airs, when she can carry her huge 600-square-foot overlapping genoa. We hoist this vast spread of canvas for the first time as we approach the Dutch coast, and *FT* starts footing through the smooth water at over $7\frac{1}{2}$ knots. The following day, as it gusts up to a strong 30 knots across the Schelde, Luke keeps all the sheets pinned in tight to see what happens. What happens is that slowly, the lee float digs in, until it is totally underwater, and as it disappears, *FT* stops dead. Sheets are let go in a hurry, the wind spills out of the sails, and she quickly comes back upright. The experiment teaches us several things—that the boat will normally give us plenty of warning when she is overcanvassed, except when she is hit by a sudden squall; and that the more of her float that she buries in the water, the more drag it will cause her, until the point when the whole float is buried and she stops altogether. In racing terms, that means that it will never pay to hold on to too much canvas for too long. Change down early.

On Easter Sunday, we set off on the first leg home. We will make for Dunkirk, we decide, so that we can enjoy a good French meal on our last night away, before hopping back across the Channel to Sandwich.

As we leave Breskens, on the Schelde, and turn left to run along the Dutch coast, it is blowing a strong force six to seven from the North. By now we are beginning to feel increasing confidence in the boat, and are anxious to test her to her extremes, to find what she will and will not do. With the wind on our starboard quarter, we hoist the big overlapping genoa, shake out all the rolls from the main, and head off on a south-westerly course. *FT* starts to move, surfing on the backs of waves, 9, 10, 11, 12 knots. She seems to be hard pressed—it is quite an effort to keep her straight, and she is shuddering with the strain of moving at these speeds. But the feeling is exhilarating, and we are quickly overhauling a Class One ocean racer that we had seen setting out ahead of us from the Schelde.

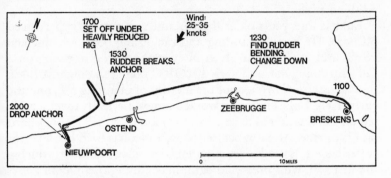

4 Chart showing *FT*'s course from Breskens to Nieuwpoort.

We have been going for an hour like this when Luke comes back from a check around the boat with the words—'You'd better take a look at the rudder.' I climb up onto the counter, put a hand on the backstay, and look down at the water tearing past the blade. As *FT* starts to mount the crest of a wave, rudder is being applied to keep her straight, and then as she sets off down the wave, more rudder is applied to prevent her broaching. On each occasion, the rudder blade is visibly bending away from the stock. It is a lifting rudder (see Fig. 19, page 175), and the blade is attached through the stock by one large bolt. A combination of the bolt and the cheeks of the stock should keep it vertical. Not only is the blade bending alarmingly but the cheeks of the rudder stock are bending with it.

We change down from number one genoa to no. 2, and our speed during the surges reduces from a normal 11 to a normal 8½ knots. But even now, we are having to fight the broaches with rudder, and the sickening bending continues.

Just past Ostend, I am at the helm, *FT* broaches, and she will not come back. I look aft over the transom, and see the rudder blade floating in the water, mercifully held onto the boat by a downhaul line. We are only two miles off a lee shore, it is

47

blowing force seven and we have no rudder. I have never been in a situation remotely like this before. We quickly take the sails off, and I start casting around for a solution to our crisis. Should we, I ask Luke, sail her straight up onto the beach a mile away? It is an idiotic question and it receives a suitably scathing reply.

Luke is four years older than I, and vastly more experienced offshore. He has been sailing and racing big boats for nineteen years, and has been involved in everything from crewing on a tall ship to regular and varied RORC racing to doing a season on a 12-metre. Throughout the months of planning *FT*, and the early trials, Luke and I had worked almost perfectly together. He left all final decisions to me. I in turn found myself leaning hard on his advice. Already before today, Luke has used his superior experience to save *FT* from an embarrassing accident—during the first sail, with press photographers aiming their zoom lenses at the boat, he noticed that the lee cap shroud—the main wire holding the mast upright—had come adrift from its fitting and was flapping in the breeze. If he had not seen it, the mast would probably have bent in two a few minutes later when we tacked.

Now, drifting towards the Dutch coast, Luke takes control. He knows what to do, and he gets on and does it. Get the anchor out, get the main warp out, drop it over in 30 feet of water, although not before I have almost lost both anchor and warp by failing to tail it properly. Back to the stern, check the damage. The nut holding the bolt that keeps the rudder blade in place has sheared, and we have no replacement. Hang over the transom, which is rearing and bucking, first dunking Luke's head in the water, then lifting him clear of it. Hang onto my legs, he calls up to me, and sets about the intricate job of reeving some 8 mm line through the bolt holes in the rudder stock, then through the hole in the blade, then again through the rudder stock, then back again, four or five times. It all takes nearly an hour, by the end of which we are both bitterly cold.

The rudder is now quite literally held together by string, and the blade, although in place, is no longer secure, and flaps about drunkenly from side to side as the several strands of line trying to perform the task of a bolt stretch to meet the pressure of the waves and sea passing by. We'll try her under storm jib

4 Foam-sandwich construction. First, you build
some light frames and stringers.

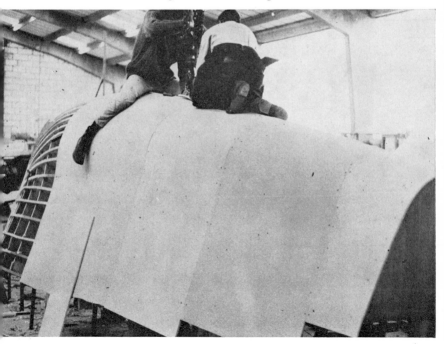

5 Then you tack on some PVC foam.

6 Next, you lay on your glass fibre.

7 Finally, you turn the whole lot upside down,
pull out all the wood, and glass the inside.

and heavily reefed main, says Luke, and I go forward to find the relevant sail—and discover that the sail locker is nine inches deep in what must be about forty gallons of water. Pump out the sail locker; check the floats, one of them is a third full, pump that out; bend on the storm jib, put twenty rolls in the main, hoist the main; winch up the anchor. Winching up the anchor takes half an hour, with Luke and I taking turns on the big genoa winch, at times putting four hands to the winch handle to inch the boat forward into the sea and wind.

At last we are off, hoping to tack back to Ostend, which is now about five miles to the north of us—dead to windward. But under our reduced sail we cannot point closer than 60 degrees to the wind, and steering does not prove very easy. Luke asks me to check for harbours of refuge further down the coast. The next harbour is Nieuwpoort, about six miles downwind, which according to the pilot book has two pile piers—nearly half a mile long—through which we must pass. 'As with other similar pier harbours, a certain amount of tidal turbulence must be expected and allowed for.'

Entering Nieuwpoort, I tell Luke, is out of the question. If we lose our rudder in or near the entrance, we shall be smashed to pieces against the piers. As if on cue, we lose our steerage again—the downhaul line, which earlier in the day saved our rudder blade for us, has worked loose, and the blade has popped up. Luke once again gets the rudder back in place, and we set off out into the North Sea, intending to spend the night as far away from land as possible.

By this time, we are both extremely tired—Luke from his exertions over the transom, and I from winching up the anchor, emptying the sail locker, and emptying the floats. We are cold, the weather shows every sign of getting worse, and the prospect of a night among the North Sea shipping lanes with a rudder held on by string, leaking floats, and not enough hot food is proving increasingly alarming. The only remotely optimistic fact that we have discovered is that with no rudder at all, *FT* will steer herself on a course due west, which means that we can get away from the Belgian shore.

Luke goes below, and I am left on deck to ponder my own gathering exhaustion and the imminent arrival of dusk. A few minutes later, he is on deck again. 'We're going to Nieuwpoort.' 'What about the rudder? Supposing the line goes?' 'Let's assume it won't, and deal with the situation if it arrives.' We turn downwind. I check our position and course. We take the mainsail right down, and most of the storm jib as well, leaving a half-hoisted storm jib—no more than 50 square feet of sail— and the windage of the boat to take us to our harbour of refuge. Even so, *FT* starts to surge down the waves at up to 8 knots. We identify Nieuwpoort, then the entrance, and finally we can see the long dark shape of a pier groping its way out to sea. As we approach it, the bottom shelves sharply, the waves become steeper. We are picked up by a wave that seems almost vertical as it comes up behind us, and we start to surf ahead of it—8, 9, 10 knots. For a few delirious seconds, with virtually no sail up at all, *FT* is surging at over 10 knots, and the entrance is now just 100 yards away. The tension between Luke and me is tangible, we both know that we cannot turn back now; we can see the waves crashing into the side of the pier and the spray being hurled up over the top of it.

And then it is all over. We are in the entrance, we are through it, in calm water. Their is a pier on either side of us, a couple of fishermen sitting on the pier are staring down at us, pipes stuck into their faces, not so much as a flicker of movement or recognition. I am shaking Luke's hand, thanking him, congratulating him, tension evaporating, I hoist the jib and a bit of main to get us into the yacht harbour.

The next day, we were on the ferry back to Dover, carrying a badly bent rudder and its stock. The list of essential items that needed looking at was growing alarmingly large—leaking floats, leaking sail locker, rudder, forward beams (we had decided to put fairings (Plate 12) on them to try and stop them hitting the water so hard when she started to pitch). Derek Kelsall came to meet us at Dover, and it was a sombre little gathering that met that evening at his home in Sandwich.

May 18: *FT*'s first race, from Cowes to Poole and back again. It is a perfect mid-May day, sun shining, sea breeze expected at any moment. Ten multihulls go to the Island Sailing Club starting line, including *British Oxygen*, at 70 feet the largest catamaran ever built. Anthony Churchill, who for the past two years has been on *Morning Cloud* with Ted Heath, is navigating, and seems to know every current in the Solent.

After twenty minutes, a gentle sea breeze comes in. It is a dead beat up to and through the Needles Channel, and *FT* revels in it. Ahead of us are about fifty monohulls, all of whom have started either 15 or 30 minutes before us. Almost immediately, *FT* starts to sail straight past them. Big boats, little boats, Class One ocean racers twice her size—she just eats them up. Just past Hurst Castle, Owen Aisher in his light green *Yeoman* tacks in front of me, and I try and pinch closer to the wind to pass him to windward. After a few minutes, I ease *FT*'s sheets and bear away to pass to leeward instead. The effect is as if I had changed down from top to third gear in a sports car. *FT* accelerates, storms through *Yeoman*'s lee, and once past, leaves her as if standing still. I do not take the sheets in again. I have just discovered another of her secrets—she likes to be sailed with her sheets eased, to be given her head and allowed to go fast. In this weather, and at the speed I am now driving her, she is pointing almost as close to the wind as all these ocean-racing monohulls. As we approach the Poole Bar buoy, with the wind now blowing a steady force four, only one monohull is still ahead of us—*Morning Cloud*, with Owen Parker at the helm.

On the way back from Poole to Cowes, *FT* and *Morning Cloud* are never more than 40 yards apart. Five times we change positions. Coming through the Hurst Narrows, we spend some twenty minutes alongside one another. Not a word is exchanged between the two crews as they both concentrate on finding a way of leaving the other behind. Just before the finish, the wind goes lighter, *FT* keeps a little bit of extra speed on, and crosses the line less than a minute ahead of *Morning Cloud*. *British Oxygen* is ahead of us, but only by twenty minutes. She had passed us at great speed just before the Poole Bar buoy. The next multihull is Bill Howell in *Tahiti Bill*, half an hour behind. We are easy handicap winners. I find myself stroking the boat, talking to her, offering her endearments. The rest of the crew look on in bemused bewilderment. For them, it has been a particularly enjoyable day's racing in a very fast boat. For me, it is far more than that. After months of wondering and worrying, I know that Derek Kelsall has designed and built me a superlative racing machine; perhaps more importantly, I have sailed an almost faultless tactical race, and got the very best out of the boat; and I have done it without Luke being there to lean on. (He has taken the weekend off.)

Before the Poole Bar race, I had been suffering agonies of self-doubt at the growing evidence of my lack of offshore experience. After it, I never really looked back again. I still had a lot to learn before I could think of setting out singlehanded across the Atlantic. But I was able to convince myself—at least most of the time—that it would all come right in the end.

June 14: The day before the Crystal Trophy. *FT* had spent yet another week at a boatyard, trying to resolve outstanding problems. By the end of last weekend, the fairings we had put on the forward lower beam to reduce the deadening impact of her pitching had broken off—they were not strong enough. The sail locker was still leaking through the point at which the lower forward beam came through the hull. There were various leaks into the main cabin, where Luke and I were going to have to spend the best part of a month with just one double bunk between us. Against this, two major problems had been solved— a heavily beefed up rudder now appeared to be up to the job of steering the boat; and the leaking into the floats was more or less over—most of the water was coming in through the chain plates, and we had devised a system to stop it, using the rubber gaiters that cover a Triumph car's gear lever.

The first few months of *FT*'s life had not been quite as I had expected. Luke kept telling me that ocean racers in their first season always have troubles. But I had not allowed for the amount of time and money that would be consumed in trying to put these troubles right.

Every weekend, I was going back to London with a list of about twenty items that needed doing. The first fifteen were easy—a visit to Captain O. M. Watts or the London Yacht Centre usually dealt with them. But the last five were guaranteed to cause problems. Where, for instance, could I find a spare compass light for a Danforth compass? It was an American compass, which would only take an American bulb. The solution to that problem involved a visit to three London yacht chandlers and a twenty-minute wait for service in each before drawing a blank; then six wasted telephone calls; finally a plea to the man at the importers' office to break all his rules and send me one direct. Total time—probably, one way and another, about eight hours. Worth it? Well, supposing the compass light did blow during the race—I had sailed through the night before with no compass light, trying to keep a torch in place, water-logging the torch, finding another torch, holding it by hand till dawn . . . It was the kind of tiny little detail that *had* to be sorted out before a major race.

Then there were the big items—big in the sense that they cost more money, and usually needed a yard to fit them. The main halyard winch was too small for the job. It had taken a month of searching through brochures and talking to other ocean racers to find an adequate replacement. The boatyard had fitted the new one that week. Would it work? On this particular day I took delivery of a device called a Spee-Squeezer, a spin-naker chute designed to make the hoisting and lowering of spinnakers easy and safe when short-handed (Plate 11). I had been looking for something like this since last October—Hood at one point was designing one for me. Then I discovered there was a man on the Isle of Wight who had invented just what I wanted. I rang him up, we had a five-minute conversation, and now, here was this spinnaker chute that I was playing with in the marina—exactly and precisely what I wanted.

Slowly, the boat was taking over my life. All week now, she was in the back of my mind, and for much of the time in the front of it. When I first launched into the transatlantic race venture, I persuaded myself that I needed something like this to complement my job, that somehow having an outside interest would enhance both my own life and the performance of my work. Now, I felt myself free-wheeling at work, and the feeling worried me.

FT had to do well in the Round Britain Race—an awful lot depended on that. Supposing I did badly? Supposing *FT* cap-sized; or was dismasted? With just three weekends to go before the start, pride, nervous tension, worries about the mounting costs of repairs, a developing feeling that I and my job and the boat and the race were inextricably bound up together, were all combining into an unwholesome mental tangle. A good result in the Crystal Trophy would help relieve some of the tension.

June 15: The Crystal Trophy is Europe's only serious multihull ocean race, sailed over a 300-mile course from Cowes to Cherbourg, then west to the Wolf Rock and back to the finish at Plymouth. This year, the race has attracted a glittering fleet, with almost all the new multihulls that have been built for the Round Britain Race competing—led by Phil Weld's 60-foot trimaran *Gulf Streamer* and Brian Cooke's big blue trimaran *Triple Arrow*. The boat I really want to beat is Nick Keig's *Three Legs of Mann*, our chief rival for the under 35-foot trophy in the Round Britain Race. She is another Kelsall design, with one season's campaigning already behind her, in many ways similar to *FT*, but six feet longer on the waterline, and therefore potentially faster. (Unlike *FT*, she was not built for the Atlantic race *Jester* trophy. It is the *Jester* rule tha thas determined *FT*'s very short 28-foot waterline.) *FT* carries a taller mast and therefore more sail area than *Three Legs*. My hunch is that *FT* will outsail her in light airs, but will not keep up with her in heavy weather.

I have picked the best crew for the race I could find. Besides Luke, there is Anthony Churchill, one of the best navigators in Britain, who had a lot to do with our victory in the Poole Bar race; and Hugh Stephenson, editor of the *Times* Business News, and one of my former partners in the Iroquois catamaran syndicate.

The night before the race, I hardly sleep. But I wake up to a beautiful windless morning, a haze over the Solent, a weather forecast of light and variable winds all day.

Just before the starting gun, the faintest zephyr of a breeze comes in from the South-east. All the fleet is kedged on the line waiting for a breeze to arrive, and we raise our kedge just in time to move up to the line on starboard tack as the gun goes. Within five minutes, *FT* is leading the fleet. After half an hour, I look behind me and find the bulk of the fleet is still becalmed inshore, including *Gulf Streamer* and *Three Legs of Mann*. Fifty yards behind us is *Trifle*, General Farrant's much-campaigned warrior, a far larger boat than *FT*, but in this breeze unable to keep up with her. This is the weather that I am coming to recognise as *FT*'s favourite—a flat sea, a light wind. Not only is she moving faster, but she is also pointing higher than *Trifle*. As for *Gulf Streamer*, *Triple Arrow*, *Three Legs*, they are literally out of sight as *FT* passes through the Forts and leaves the glistening Solent behind her. Pride mixed with relief and sheer joy intoxicate me. In this weather nobody can beat *FT*.

By mid-afternoon, however, what little wind there ever was has gone. *FT* sits wallowing in a hole in the wind, and we watch one boat after another emerge out of the haze behind us and first catch up and then overhaul us.

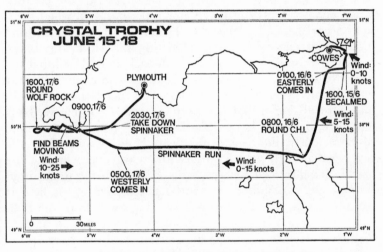

5 The Crystal Trophy, June 15–18.

A light easterly arrives during the night, and we close reach across to Cherbourg. As we round the Cherbourg buoy, shortly after breakfast, we see two sails, apparently belonging to larger boats, about two miles ahead of us. Then, just after we have rounded, *Triple Arrow* appears out of the haze behind us. We draw the conclusion—correctly as it turns out—that the two sails ahead of us are the two leaders and that they must be

Gulf Streamer and *Trifle*. After the first eighty miles, we are lying third, and well ahead on corrected time of all those boats in sight of us.

The long 170-mile haul to the Wolf Rock is punctuated by calms and fog. Progress is painfully slow, often non-existent, the kind of weather where you always assume that your rivals have found wind when you have none. On Monday morning, an honest westerly comes in, force four to five, we tack in towards the shore and find we are just east of the Lizard, about 30 miles to the Wolf Rock—in this wind, and with a foul tide about to hit us, probably five or six hours sailing.

Half way through the morning, I am suddenly aware of a noise that has been there for some time, but is growing in intensity. As *FT* rises and falls to the waves, there is a creaking and groaning sound coming from somewhere in the cockpit. I talk about it with Anthony Churchill, who is on watch with me, and neither of us can find it. Then Anthony feels something move—it is one of the bolts attaching the aft beam to the cockpit bulkhead. I move into the aft cockpit, and find that the whole of the aft beam assembly is alive. The eight bolts that hold the top beam to the bulkhead—and therefore to the main hull—are all loose, and the beam is working sideways, back and forth, back and forth, about a quarter of an inch at a time. More seriously, the back of the beam is lifting away from the hull, so that each time *FT* dives into a wave and brakes, the mast is being thrown forward, a shock load is being transmitted through the cap shrouds to the float, the stern of the float is tending to lift, and the beam is twisting away from the hull. My first reaction is to take everything down and limp back to Plymouth. I wake Luke up; his instinct is all the other way—keep going somehow, we cannot just throw the race away. Get out the wrench, tighten up all those bolts, as long as they are there, the beam cannot leave the boat unless the whole bulkhead breaks in half and that is most unlikely to happen. By now, the Wolf Rock lighthouse is in sight, a dark finger on the horizon, so we press on, tightening the bolts every half hour, trying to ignore the ever louder noise coming from the beam as it lifts further and further from the deck. As we approach the Wolf Rock, it starts to blow a solid force six, we have too much sail up, I am spilling wind on the main, feathering during the squalls. Anthony mutters almost to himself, 'I never knew you could press a multihull like this.' We are at the Rock, easing our sheets, heading back for Plymouth with the wind behind us. Everything is suddenly calm, we are surging down the waves at a comfortable 8 knots, there is no more creaking from the aft beam, the boat feels safe again.

Luke and I both agree that in this wind we cannot put up the spinnaker—three weekends ago, we put it up in the Solent in a force seven, and felt as if our stern was about to be lifted out of the water. Instead, we will put up the no. 2 genoa and goosewing it. Up it goes, on goes the spinnaker pole—but *FT* fails to respond. Seven and a half knots, sometimes 8, an occasional $8\frac{1}{2}$-knot surge—she should be going much faster with a 24-knot wind dead behind her. Luke and I look at each other and shake our heads. We dare not risk it. Why not? Now's the time to try it if we are ever going to, with four people on board and a race to win. I go forward and pump out the sail locker— still leaking a bit. Then, both the kedges, the two heaviest sails and the rubber dinghy are lugged to the stern, to bring as much weight aft as possible. We reef the main. As an added precaution, I raise the centreboard to reduce the risk of broaching. Up goes the spinnaker inside its chute, on goes the boom. A glance at Luke—we both grin, neither of us really knows what is going to happen. But Luke is on the spinnaker sheet, the one that will need to be let go quickly if we get into trouble. I start lifting the spinnaker chute, the spinnaker starts to fill, the chute bucket slides to the top of the sail, the spinnaker billows, and the little trimaran takes off: 10, 11, 12 knots. Far from threatening to bury her bows, the faster she goes, the further her bows lift out of the water. Kelsall has given her a vast volume of buoyancy forward, both in the main hull and the floats, and she is riding over the following sea. A couple of times, she broaches, but when she does, the spinnaker just collapses, she slides sideways, and shows no sign of burying her float or of wanting to flip. We are having to use a lot of rudder—it is an effort to keep her straight. But the sensation of speed and stability is exhilarating. She surges to 13 knots; then to 14. Off the Lizard, we sail straight through some race water. I fight with the wheel to keep her on course, she climbs on the back of a particularly steep wave and sets off down its face chasing the next one, the speedometer rises to 15, for a few seconds to $15\frac{1}{2}$ knots. After the Lizard, we keep heading due east so that we can carry our spinnaker for yet another hour. When we take it down, with thirty miles of broad reach ahead of us, we put up our 600-square-foot light-weather genoa. *FT* again responds magnificently. More 12- and 13-knot surges, Luke and Hugh Stephenson start talking about catching the midnight train from Plymouth. Anthony Churchill, meanwhile, has gone to sleep— curled up in the aft cockpit, lying on the two anchors. It is his first sleep since Cowes, $2\frac{1}{2}$ days earlier.

Just off Rame Head, five miles from the finish, the sea churns up again, I find myself fighting to keep her straight as she mounts a wave, burying the bow of her lee float on the way up it. She reaches the top, feels it underneath her, surges down the far side, a final fifteen-knot burst before settling back to the relative calm of Plymouth Sound and the finishing line. We cross the finish a few seconds after midnight. We have done the 71 miles from the Wolf Rock in eight hours, some of it with the tide against us. Allowing for the time it took to get the spinnaker up and for the foul tide, we have probably averaged 10 knots over 65 miles through the water since the spinnaker was hoisted. By any standards, that is a remarkable performance for a little boat with just 28 feet on her waterline.

The following morning we discover that only three boats—all much larger—have finished ahead of us: *Gulf Streamer*, *Triple Arrow* and *Trifle*. We have beaten *Three Legs of Mann* by $5\frac{1}{2}$ hours. By mid-morning, I know we have won the Crystal Trophy—none of the boats still at sea can beat us. Derek Kelsall is in Plymouth for the finish, and comes aboard to examine the beams. We should tie the back of the top beam to the back of the bottom one with two stainless steel straps, he suggests. Since the bottom beam is fixed through the hull, that should cure the lifting problem. To solve the loose bolts, get Mashfords yard to put Locktite on all of them to stop them working loose again. Over to Mashfords, where the boat is booked in to be slipped before the race. Long list of jobs for Mashfords. Even longer list of jobs to be done in London. Back to the Royal Western, one of the friendliest and most charming clubs in Britain, where a party is already in progress. This victory in the Crystal Trophy has lifted an enormous weight off my mind. We have drawn first blood with *Three Legs*. *FT* is going to be all right. With a modicum of luck, we can win our class in the Round Britain Race.

Back to London on the overnight sleeper with a holdall full of silver. Some time that week—neither of us can any longer remember when—Elizabeth and I sit out in the garden of my house in Islington sipping wine and decide to get married. We have been talking about it since Christmas. We will do it over August Bank Holiday weekend. The following weekend we spend drawing up lists and writing out envelopes. It is only the third weekend I have spent at home since March, and the first when I have not been working on the Sunday.

4

THE ROUND BRITAIN RACE

FIRST LEG. PLYMOUTH TO CROSSHAVEN, JULY 6–8

July 6: At 11.30 a.m. a cannon booms out across Plymouth Sound. Sixty-one yachts, including 21 multihulls, edge up to the starting line, in almost windless conditions, trying to avoid each other and the vast spectator fleet. A light south-westerly reaches the Sound about five minutes after the starting gun. Very soon, after a couple of narrow shaves with spectator boats, *FT* is through the western entrance and heading for the Eddystone Light, the first mark of the course. Ahead of us are *Gulf Streamer* and *Three Cheers*, the two Newick-designed trimarans, both going about a knot faster. Down to leeward is *Burton Cutter*, at 80 feet overall the largest boat in the race, rolling around like a heavyweight boxer, not enjoying the light airs one bit. To windward is *Quailo III*, a veteran of both the British Admiral's Cup and Southern Cross teams, a gleaming, spotless Class One ocean racer, pointing a good 5 degrees closer to the wind than we are, and slowly pulling away from us. On our weather quarter, and going at about the same speed, is *Slithy Tove*, light blue blotchy paint, old stained sails, but nevertheless a beautiful-looking boat, long, light, thin and graceful, with a bulb keel slung underneath her. She is sailed by her owner-designer, Michael Pipe, the man who two winters back I had tried and failed to find when we were first planning *FT*.

And behind us is *Three Legs of Mann*. Luke and I made a marginally better start than Nick and Peter Keig, and broke away from the main fleet and the spectator boats just ahead of them. Now, she is 40 yards behind and to leeward of us, and we are going at exactly the same speed, and pointing in exactly the same direction. For two hours we sail like this—*Three Legs* catches us, then we pull ahead of her, then she catches us again. Throughout, we are never more than 50 yards apart.

T's COURSE ROUND BRITAIN

60 MILES

Wind: 10-20knots

0300, 18/7
MUCKLE FLUGGA

0500, 17/7
GUDGEON BREAKS.
RUDDER LOST

Lerwick
BEAMS FOUND
TO BE CRACKED

Wind: 25-30knots

SUN-SIGHT
U-BOLT BREAKS

SULE SKERRY

BUTT OF LEWIS

Wick

E TO NORTH-
ERLY GALE

0930, 15/7
ST. KILDA

1400, 21/7
WICK REPORTS
FORCE NINE

Wind: 25-35knots

Castlebay

W E S T E R L Y   G A L E S

0800, 12/7

nots.

0100, 23/7
WIND CHANGE

Dudgeon
Lightship

Wind:
10-15
knots

EAGLE ISLAND
BLACK ROCK

1200, 23/7
BECALMED

Wind
5-15
knots

FIRST SIGHTING
OF QUAILO

Cromer
Lowestoft

Crosshaven

7/
.LIG

DNIGHT 10/7
STNET ROCK

1200, 26/7

7/7, 2030
GUDGEON BREAKS

PLYMOUTH
START →
JULY 6, 1130

1200, 27/7

7/7, 1200
BISHOP ROCK

FINISH
JULY 28, 1744

Wind:
18-30knots

Wind:
5-20knots

6 *FT*'s course Round Britain.

It is thrilling racing, just like a dinghy race in Chichester Harbour, but this time, we have nearly 1,900 miles ahead of us. After two hours, the wind pipes up to force four, the sea becomes a little shorter, and *FT* starts to pitch. Soon, *Three Legs* is through us and away, and after another hour has vanished into the haze.

The wind dies again, and shortly after nightfall, a thick fog comes in. *FT* ghosts through the night, maintaining a good speed throughout. At breakfast on Sunday, the fog lifts to show me my first view of the Scillies in my life, a succession of green lumps in the sunlight. We round the Bishop Rock lighthouse, without another boat in sight, and set course for Crosshaven on the southern coast of Ireland. We hoist the spinnaker and settle down for a gentle day with the wind behind us, heading slightly to windward of our rhumb line to keep our speed up. It is a beautiful, sunny, warm, peaceful day's sailing, only slightly marred by the discovery that the self-steering device that has been fitted in Plymouth does not work. It is the second we have tried this year. We are going to have to be at the helm the whole way round the course.

At eight o'clock, with the evening beginning to close in, and a slight increase in wind forecast for the night, I come up from fours hours' sleep to take over the helm. 'Steering's a bit stiff,' Luke reports. I cook a meal, most of which Luke rejects—he has a migraine headache, and takes a couple of aspirin before putting his head down. The steering *is* odd. First it is stiff; then it feels as if it is not there at all. After half an hour, I step onto the counter to look at the rudder. It is lurching about from side to side. One of the two gudgeons that fix it to the transom has broken clean off. It is now only attached to the top of the transom, held in place by the action of the steering wires on the tiller. The unfair strains on the top gudgeon are considerable. There is an imminent danger that it too will break off.

I wake a white-faced Luke, who surveys the damage. His head is throbbing, and he is in no state to do anything other than steer. I gather up every spare piece of rope I can find, and begin what turns out to be a long night hanging over the transom. By wrapping rope as tightly as I can round the rudder stock, then feeding it through the pintle, I can reduce the amount of swing on the blade a little. But the forces acting on the blade are intense—far greater than my strength. I have to wait until the sea pushes the blade one way or another before threading a piece of line behind the stock, and several times my fingers are nearly caught by a sudden violent movement. After two hours, now in pitch darkness and working by torch-light, I have rigged up a cat's cradle of lines, attaching the back of the rudder to the pintle and to the stainless steel straps holding the bumpkin in place. The rudder is still swinging, but the ropes are limiting the swing to a couple of inches either way. Luke goes back to the bunk looking extremely unwell. The wind has strengthened, and *FT*, still under spinnaker, is making a steady 9 knots, at one point surging up to 11, as a light sea is put up by the rising breeze. At 1.00 a.m. I feel the rudder go again. Every one of my lines has chafed through. Luke comes back on deck, we down spinnaker as rapidly as possible, and try to keep our speed down. But the wind has increased, we are making over 7 knots under mainsail only. We heave to briefly while I reeve another cat's cradle round the rudder stock, then set off again for Crosshaven. Every twenty minutes one of the lines chafes through and needs replacing. Each time I do it, it takes me longer, as lack of sleep begins to catch up.

At last dawn arrives, a grey, drizzling, dank Irish dawn. If only we can make Crosshaven. It is just 10 miles away now, we have picked up the Daunt light vessel on the RDF, and we are still ahead of the bad weather that is forecast. All night, I have been willing that rudder to stay attached to the boat until Crosshaven. If it comes away, the race is lost. Luke and I start trying to work out what has happened. It must be another manifestation of the trouble we had at Easter. For some reason, the rudder is a fundamental weakness in the design of the boat. Having beefed up the weakest point, we have transferred the damage to the next weakest link in the chain. But when did we do it? Throughout the first day, we were in almost windless conditions. The Crystal. Of course. We broke it during the Crystal. I remember that final 15-knot burst off Rame Head, in pitch darkness just before the finish, when I had to fight to keep her straight. The weld that has now sheared clean off must have all but gone in those seconds. But it held to the finish of the Crystal; it held throughout the first day of this race; yesterday afternoon, more in sorrow than in anger, it gave up the ghost. If only we can make Crosshaven.

At 7.00 a.m. on Monday July 8, the green headlands of Ireland begin looming out of the mist. Luke was born and brought up in Ireland and recognises Roche Point, our finishing line for this leg of the course. We steer at it, still carrying a heavily reefed main to try and reduce the pressure on the rudder. Out of the mist looms a sail, another trimaran. For five minutes we train the binoculars on it, I wish for it to be *Three Legs*. But it is *Croda Way*, another rival in the under 35-foot class, 100 yards ahead of us after nearly two days sailing. We must beat her across the finish—up goes the no. 2 genoa, out go the rolls from the main. To no avail, she beats us by just under a minute. As we round the point to enter Crosshaven Harbour, we are greeted by an array of multihulls lying at anchor—*Three Cheers, British Oxygen, Triple Arrow, Gulf Streamer, Three Legs of Mann*. *FT* is lying seventh, third in her class. But where are *Burton Cutter, Quailo*? Where for that matter is *Manureva*, Alain Colas's magnificent trimaran that started the race as favourite? None has arrived. Multihulls have taken the first seven places. *British Oxygen*, the big, red 70-foot catamaran, is lying first, just over an hour ahead of the much smaller trimaran *Three Cheers*. *Three Legs*, lying fifth overall, is just two hours ahead of *FT*—roughly what we reckon we have lost with our rudder problems. Our spirits rise. We have made Crosshaven, we still have everything to play for.

SECOND LEG. CROSSHAVEN TO CASTLE BAY, JULY 10–13

July 10: The forty-eight-hour compulsory stopover in Crosshaven was filled with worry over the boat. The yard rewelded the gudgeon to the rudder—'that there weld will last for ever,' I was promised in cheerful Irish brogue. We removed a couple of Talurit splices from the standing rigging and replaced them with Norseman terminals—the standing rigging, particularly

8 The final design meeting at my house. L. to R.: Luke FitzHerbert, the author and his wife, Derek Kelsall, Ralph Farrant, Peter Dove and Terry Pearce.

9 Lady Drogheda names this boat *FT*, March 1974.

10 *FT*'s first sail off Ramsgate, March 1974. Note the join of the two metal cross beams, and the positioning of the gusset plate. Note too how water is spilling out of the lower beam, and how close is the flat forward edge of this beam to the water. A thin aluminium sheet roof was laid over the beam to prevent it filling with water, and fairings were fitted on its forward edge to try to dampen the shock when it hit a wave.

11 *FT* off Bembridge, April 1976. The chute and bucket of the 'Spee-Squeezer' have been hoisted to the top of the mast. take the spinnaker down, the wind must be let out of the sai and then the bucket and chute will be pulled down over the spinnaker. Note the position of liferaft and safety box on aft si of rear beams, accessible if boa capsized. (*Freddie Mansfield*)

the inner forestay, was taking a succession of shock loads when *FT* beat into a sea, and this job was a precautionary measure. When the race was over, almost all the other competitors were to look back on Crosshaven as the high point—the Irish hospitality, the last time when all the fleet was together in one place, the beauty of Crosshaven. For me, it was a period of great tension. I was literally worrying myself sick—nervous tension and tiredness combined to seize up the muscles in my shoulders into what the local doctor called fibrositic nodules. I am not sure what they are, but they caused great pain across the back and up the neck, and on the morning of July 10, I woke with one of those headaches that seems to press in on the whole of the skull. The tension that I had been generating around me proved too much for Luke. On the second day in Crosshaven, he fled to stay with friends.

This morning, it is wet and grey and miserable. We are supposed to be out at our starting line at 7.16 a.m.—exactly 48 hours after our arrival. I have left it too late, and the only mild consolation is that *Croda Way* has left it even later—she is motoring out about half a mile behind us. The wind is in the West—a dead beat to the Fastnet Rock, which we have to round. The course instructions state simply that we must round all the British Isles except the Channel Islands and Rockall. For those purposes, the Fastnet Rock represents a British Isle.

'I should put up the no. 3 if I were you.' Luke wants to be cautious; I want to be daring. Up goes the no. 2, and off we set. Within minutes it is obvious we are carrying too much sail. Up to the foredeck, change the sail, back again. *Croda Way* has slipped past us, I have wasted a lot of energy, and soaked myself through to the skin. I should have listened to Luke.

All that day, we beat westwards, with the wind gradually freshening. In mid-morning, a light blue shape emerges out of the mist, rising to the waves, slicing through them. It is *Slithy Tove*, long and graceful, going a good 25 per cent. faster than we. She started over an hour behind us, but has quickly made up the difference.

At midday, the mist lifts, the rain leaves us, the wind continues to blow force six to seven. But we have discovered that by dipping into each of the bays along Ireland's south coast, we can stay in more or less flat water. All day, we dodge in and out of them, carrying a makeshift cutter rig—a new yankee jib that Hood delivered the week before the race, and the storm staysail on the inner forestay, with the main well reefed. It is not an ideal combination, and not one for which the boat was designed. But the smallest of her regular headsails is too big for this wind, even in the smooth water. This cutter rig—an invention of Luke's—just has to do.

We round the Fastnet Rock at midnight—it has taken us a tiresome 17 hours to get there, an average speed of only $3\frac{1}{2}$ knots. By 9 a.m. on July 11, we are at the Great Skellig lighthouse and easing our sheets for the long push up the west coast of Ireland. The wind is westerly, force five to six. All that day, we press northwards, no. 2 genoa and full main up, the needle reading 8 to $8\frac{1}{2}$ knots. Over the following 24 hours, we average 8 knots and do just under 200 miles. It is to be our fastest and most enjoyable leg of the race. At about midday on the second day, half way up the Irish coast, *Manureva* comes up from behind us, travelling at about 11 knots, Alain Colas sitting impassively at the helm, the big trimaran slopping over the waves. Colas and *Manureva*—the most famous sailing partnership in the world. They have sailed together for 80,000 miles, and have broken every record they have attempted. It is a pleasure to be overtaken by such a boat, as she drives through our lee and heads for the horizon. But Colas is not going to win this race—*Manureva* is heavily over-weight, and Colas took the first leg far too easily.

In mid-afternoon, *Quailo III*, the only real thoroughbred ocean racer in the whole fleet of 61 boats, heaves into view, half a mile away from us on our port beam. It is the beginning of a race that lasts for the next 36 hours. Every time the wind goes a little ahead of the beam, *Quailo*, with her $39\frac{1}{2}$ feet of waterline and heavy displacement, inches ahead. Whenever the wind backs to aft of the beam, *FT* slides past *Quailo*.

At dusk, *Quailo* is pulling away from us as the wind moves slightly north of East. But the following day, having cleared Black Rock and Eagle Island in the small hours of the morning, we overhaul *Quailo* again, and again start racing each other, changing positions all day. With sunset approaching, the dark and brooding shape of Barra Head comes up ahead of us. As it

66

does so, the wind begins to die, and backs through 10 degrees, and we start edging away from *Quailo*. Darkness sets in and *Quailo*'s lights recede behind us, until we can no longer see them. Our little private race is won—at least for this leg.

As we approach the entrance to Castle Bay harbour, we pass too close to a mass of rock known as Muldoanich and lose our wind. We drift past Muldoanich, and beat towards the finishing line. The wind is all over the place, and I make two bad tacks. With 50 yards to go, I look over my shoulder. *Quailo*'s lights are moving fast up behind me. She has held her speed past Muldoanich, and is pointing high towards the finishing line. I tack onto starboard, and force her to tack too. I try and hold her on past the line, so that I can tack back onto port and cross ahead of her. But she points too high, she just steers across my bow. Two more tacks, both faultlessly executed, and *Quailo* crosses the line 15 seconds ahead of us. Where else in the world would two boats as totally different as *Quailo*, the thoroughbred ocean racer, and *FT*, the brash little trimarin, have a race like this—for 36 hours we have been within a few miles of each other.

It was 1 a.m. when we crossed the line. Within seconds, a cheerful Scottish voice was booming at us through the darkness. Yes, we would like a tow in. No, this Scotsman took no sleep during the Round Britain Race. If he went to sleep, he might not be here to greet somebody when they arrived. What of *Three Legs of Mann*? She had arrived in the middle of yesterday afternoon, $9\frac{1}{2}$ hours ahead of us. With her longer waterline, she had averaged $7\frac{3}{4}$ knots to *FT*'s 7 over the 460 miles from Crosshaven. *Manureva*, *Burton Cutter*, *Slithy Tove* and *Quailo* had all overtaken us. But *Croda Way* was still at sea. *FT* was lying tenth, second in the under 35-foot class. *Croda Way*, now third of the small boats, was eleven hours behind us, having broken a centreboard on the beat to the Fastnet Rock. At the front of the fleet, *British Oxygen* and the remarkable *Three Cheers* had put up identical times for this leg, and were still first and second, with two more big trimarans, *Triple Arrow* and *Gulf Streamer*, snapping at their heels.

I spent some time in Castle Bay pondering the race. The last leg had provided us with a thrilling tussle with *Quailo*—she was not in our class, and therefore strictly speaking not a competitor. But all through the fleet these private little races were taking place between boats of differing shapes and sizes, with the 48-hour stopovers allowing plenty of time for crews to relive the legs and make friends with their rivals. *FT*'s sail up the West Coast of Ireland, too, had been exciting.

But I felt a strange and disquieting sense of let-down, of unfulfilled expectations. Partly, it was the realisation that *Three Legs*, with her extra six feet of waterline, was a faster all-round boat than *FT*, and that we were unlikely to catch her. Partly, it was the physical discomforts—on the Crosshaven to Castle Bay leg, I had felt seasick most of the time, and the pills that I had been stuffing into myself to overcome the feeling had themselves been making me feel parched and dehydrated; I had been living in soaking clothes, and sleeping in a dripping wet sleeping bag—*FT* was proving a wet ride both outside and in; my hands were covered in cuts that would not heal—every tiny cut, as soon as it was exposed to salt water, opened up again, allowing my gloves quite literally to rub more salt into the wound.

None of this would have mattered very much if we had been winning. But the responsibility for the boat, the need to do well, were weighing me down. The rudder on the first leg was a big blow. On the second leg, the beams started to come alive again. The top forward beam was moving sideways, gently back and forth all the time. As I lay in my sleeping bag, I had to listen to it creaking. There was a serious leak into the main cabin on the port side, where the aluminium pole that carries the jib sheet track joins the hull, and another one through the cabin hatch, right above the bunk. The sail locker had started to fill with water again—the working of the top beam was letting the sea in where the beam entered the hull. The aft compartment had filled with water on the last leg, too. We had to keep a closer watch on that, pump it every few hours. We did not have the right sail configuration for going to windward in anything over force six.

In Castle Bay, I watched the crew of *Three Cheers*—Mike McMullen and Martin Read—carefree, setting off on picnics, enjoying themselves, while I worked round the boat, tightening all the nuts that held the beams to the bulkheads, trying to fill

68

the leaks, knowing even as I did so that my filler would not last more than a few hours.

The intensity of my ambition to do well in this race, to prove the boat, to prove myself (which? both, but more of the second than I was at this point able to admit) was making life difficult for Luke. He told me during the last leg that winning the race was not the reason he was doing it. He wanted to sail fast round Britain, and enjoy it. The remark angered me. Could he not understand how important it was to win? The relationship between us was beginning to grow tetchy—I overanxious, unwilling to take advice, feeling the full responsibility of sailing my employer's boat; he more relaxed, more experienced, trying to keep the peace, but reacting with increasing irritability to my overflow of nervous tension; a certain reluctance on both our parts to give way gracefully to the other. I had been warned during the winter by Glin Bennet that this race placed enormous strains on even the closest friendships. Dr Glin Bennet is a member of the department of mental health at Bristol University and has done extensive research into the consequences of fatigue at sea. 'In mental terms, it's worse than the single-handed race,' he told me. In the first race in 1966, there was a celebrated case of a skipper sailing into a harbour in Northern France, dropping his crew, and completing the course on his own. During this race, the same was to happen again when Martin Wills and Colin Hoare fell out on *Tower Casper*, and Wills completed nearly two-thirds of the course on his own. Several more crews retired rather than carry on sailing together.

Luke and I never came near to that point. We talked over the problem during the winter, and again after a particularly frustrating sail together earlier in the season. We were both well aware of the dangers and determined to avoid them. Nevertheless, the relationship had grown edgy. I wanted to catch *Three Legs*, I wanted the boat to stop falling apart. The next leg—420 miles through water into which only fishermen normally venture, round Muckle Flugga, the northernmost tip of the British Isles—the next leg had to be a light-weather one.

THIRD LEG. CASTLE BAY TO LERWICK, JULY 15–18

July 14: Before dark, we are towed out to lie at anchor in the lee of Muldoanich for our 1 a.m. start. The wind has been blowing up all day from the South-east. Luke goes to lie down, and I wait up for the 0030 weather forecast. When it comes, it is one of those really grim ones that you almost wish you had not heard. There is a low on its way. Every single shipping area in Britain has a gale warning out. For the next few days, we are to be in sea areas Hebrides and Fair Isle. The gales in the Hebrides during the next 24 hours will be from the North-east, precisely the direction in which we want to go. So much for the light-weather leg I have been dreaming of.

I am anxious to start on time tonight, especially as I know *Quailo* is just 15 seconds ahead of us. Somehow it is not to be. We are several minutes late, I am enraged at our incompetence, Luke is showing irritation at my irritation, the atmosphere on board is thoroughly unconducive to setting out into a gale. In the general melee, I gybe *FT* by mistake, the boom cracks me on the head, and my temper reaches new heights of unpleasantness. *Quailo*, meanwhile, has arrived at the starting line dead on time, and is already away and round Muldoanich.

Eventually we are on our way, under reefed main and staysail. Luke sails and I navigate the ten miles south to Barra Head, which we round just after dawn, at 3 a.m. The wind is moving round from South-east to East, freshening as it backs, blowing force six to seven as we bear away round Barra Head for the dash to some British Isles called St Kilda—a group of lonely rocks covered in birds 70 miles north-north-west of Barra. The wind is on our quarter to begin with. We will hoist our no. 1 genoa and reef the main. On the Crystal Trophy race a month ago, during that spinnaker run from the Wolf Rock back to Plymouth, we decided that the mainsail far more than the spinnaker was causing us to broach. We calculate now that with the big genoa drawing—600 square feet of sail—we can afford four rolls in the main.

Up goes the genoa; in comes the sheet. *FT* begins to fly. Fourteen and 15 knots, we are surging up to these speeds on every second wave. When a gust hits us from behind, the lee float digs into the wave ahead of us, we bear away to meet the gust, and then the lee float is up on the wave, *FT* is lifting out of the water, surging forwards. Soon we are up with *Quailo*, yelling and waving at Don Parr and Steve Allinson, both of whom have come on deck to watch the great *FT* surfing show. As we pass *Quailo*, *Peter Peter*, a large and ungainly 48-foot catamaran, who started this leg 40 minutes behind us, catches up and threatens to pass. We redouble our efforts, I on the helm, Luke on the sheet, ready to let go at the slightest warning. Luke brings the genoa sheet in a few inches, we catch a wave just right, the speedometer is up to $15\frac{1}{2}$ knots, touching 16, it is over 16 knots. We hold it there for five or ten seconds, and briefly surge ahead of *Peter Peter* again. In three full seasons' sailing, this is the fastest I ever take *FT*, and the fastest she will probably ever go. We ease the sheets, I take two more rolls on the main, and we settle back to a more comfortable surging speed of $14\frac{1}{2}$ knots, allowing *Peter Peter* to pass us. Meanwhile the wind is still backing, still increasing. I try to go below to get some sleep, knowing that this joyful abandon will be short-lived. But as I lie on the bunk, the noise is overwhelming. The whole boat is shaking, water is surging past just 4 inches from my head on the other side of the foam-sandwich skin, the hull is crashing into and over waves. Sleep is impossible.

After $6\frac{1}{2}$ hours we sail under the lee of St Kilda just before 9.30 a.m. We have sailed 70 miles at an average speed of 11 knots. It is a sail neither Luke nor I will ever forget. Whenever we see each other or talk on the phone, the dash to St Kilda always somehow comes up. John Perry, owner and skipper of *Peter Peter*, will never forget it either. John lives a charmed life at sea. He falls overboard, misreads lighthouse signals, forgets his charts; on the leg from Crosshaven, he forgot to put one of his drain plugs in place, and found his boat half full of water. That in turn waterlogged his batteries, and he sailed the whole leg with no electricity. Before the Round Britain Race is over, he is to lose his mast not once but twice (after that he will retire). But even John Perry watched us with awe as we drove *FT* at 16 knots, trying to keep up with him. He looked at the over 800 square feet of sail we were carrying and the size of our boat, and just waited for us to cartwheel. Twice, Luke did have to let go of the genoa sheet to bring *FT*'s lee float up. We were indeed driving her close to her limits, learning what those limits were. Once again we learned, as we had in the Crystal Trophy, that the great volume of buoyancy in *FT*'s bows made her a very stable boat indeed when she was being blown from behind.

At 10.10 on Monday July 15, we come out from under the lee of St Kilda. Muckle Flugga, the northernmost tip of the Shetland Islands, is 310 miles away, more or less due north-east. We are met by a force seven from the East-north-east, rising all the time, backing slowly. We set off under our makeshift cutter rig, painting roughly north. *FT* is being thrown around, rising to the waves like a seal to a fish, the wind catching her bows and blowing her off their tops. We are edging forwards at 4 to 4½ knots, but as the wind catches *FT*'s bows and blows them sideways into the next wave, she is being brought up with a start, her speed falling to under 3 knots before she regains speed and direction again. We take down the yankee jib, take some more rolls into the main. That just leaves us with a storm staysail and a main up. But this is weather with which *FT* cannot compete. Her tall and heavy mast—47 feet of it—her long floats, her great 26-foot beam all respresent a vast area of weight and windage sitting on a tiny 28-foot waterline. To move forward in this kind of sea, you need a long narrow hull with a heavy keel underneath it which will slice through the waves and keep moving forwards. *FT* is at the very opposite extreme—light, wide, lacking forward drive from her sail plan.

I am determined to keep going, willing the boat on towards Muckle Flugga. The seas are now fiercely steep—Don Parr of *Quailo* later described them as the steepest he had ever seen. The wind speed is hovering between 35 and 40 knots, gale force. As *FT* rises to a wave, and then rolls back towards the next one, the windward float is slamming the water, lifting spray off it which is picked up by the wind, and blown into my eyes and face. My eyes are stinging with the force of the spray, water is trickling down my neck and through my clothes; down below, Luke is listening to the boat taking a terrible pounding. I have some diving goggles on board, and put them on to try and protect my eyes. 'We should heave to. We are getting nowhere, and risking the boat.' I explode at Luke for the suggestion. We are racing. We have to get to Muckle Flugga. How can he suggest stopping?

Luke takes over the watch and I go below to a crescendo of noise—the bottom beam crashing into each new wave, jarring the whole boat which shudders in sympathy; the creaking of the front beam as it works to and fro; the bunk and sleeping bag already sopping wet from the various leaks. My head is singing too, from that crack from the boom in the early hours of the morning; I feel sick, tired, depressed. We hit a particularly sharp wave all wrong, there is a great blast as the boat slams back into the water, the whole hull trembles. Luke is insisting that we stop. I reluctantly submit.

Luke suggests we heave to under main only, with several more rolls in, the main let off on the sheet, and the helm left hard over. Down comes the storm jib; more rolls in the main; let out the main sheet; lash down the helm. We find ourselves lying at 65 degrees to the wind. All is suddenly peaceful, *FT* no longer trying to move forwards, but acting as a great raft to the seas, beckoning them on, and allowing them to pass under her. Waves which a few minutes ago were full of threat and pain and danger have suddenly lost their menance and their venom. It is 3 p.m., five hours since we left St Kilda.

The gale has not quite beaten me. Ninety minutes later, I think I detect a slackening in the wind. Luke and I argue over whether we should set off again, but I ignore his advice. Back into wet clothes; back into oilskins; onto the foredeck; pump out the sail locker; up with the staysail; set off again. The wind has not slackened. It is still blowing almost a gale. For the second time, we heave to. I go below, lie out on the bunk alongside Luke, and collapse in total exhaustion.

July 16, 5 a.m.: I wake up, look at my watch. I have been asleep for ten hours. I have been vaguely conscious during the night of Luke getting up to check things. Water is slopping around on the floor of the cabin, there is a general air of damp and wet. Both of us get up, I pump the bilges dry, Luke checks the wind and sea conditions. The wind has continued to back, as forecast. It is still blowing force seven, showing 30 knots on

73

the dial, but we may be able to point in roughly the direction we want to go. Soggy jeans, wet sweaters. The unkindest cut of all is the wet necktowel, the piece of clothing that is supposed to stop water running down my body. Before wrapping it round my neck, I have to wring the water out of it. Back into wet oilskins. The cuts on my hands have all dried up overnight into raw sores, my fingers feel stiff. Gently, I pull gloves over my hands. We both nibble at biscuits and throw back some soup before attaching our safety harness lines and stepping back on deck.

Pump out the sail locker and stern locker. Go out to the floats, lift off the hatches, check them for water—they are neither of them too bad, but require a short spell of pumping. Set the storm staysail. Half an hour after coming on deck we are off again. The wind is just west of north, and is moderating. The glass is beginning to show signs of wanting to go up. We plug on into the sea, hoping that *FT* can take what we are asking of her. We are just about heading north-east, the direction in which we want to go.

Early in the season Luke had expressed grave doubts at the ability of *FT*'s rig to hold her long and heavy deck-stepped mast in place. Slightly to his surprise, the mast is still standing. But as *FT* rises and falls to the sea, the mast pants, springing fore and aft, and as it does so, it transmits severe shock loads onto the inner forestay. At lunchtime, the U-bolt holding the inner forestay to the deck breaks in two. We heave to for 45 minutes, Luke standing in the sail locker armed with a monkey wrench, a mole wrench, a hacksaw and several pairs of pliers. Fifty minutes later, we are off again. Another breakage. Another weakness that needs looking at.

While we are hove to, the sun has come out for the first time on this leg, and I have got a midday sunsight. I now start, gingerly, to work the figures out. It is the first sight I have ever taken in earnest, almost the first time I have handled my new sextant. I look up tables, check my figures, double check everything, and then with some nervousness draw a line on the chart. I am astonished to find that we are 30 miles further north than I have been estimating. That cannot be right. I start tuning into the surrounding radio beacons. There is the Butt of Lewis,

60 miles away, rather faint; and here is Sule Skerry over 100 miles away, but surprisingly clear. They all point to the same conclusion. We *are* 30 miles further north, 30 miles nearer our objective, than I had been estimating.

How come? I have assumed, in arriving at our dead reckoning (DR) position, that we were blown back about 18 miles in the course of our 12 hours hove to. Instead, exactly the opposite appears to have happened. While hove to, we had left our centre-board down, with our heavily rolled mainsail fixed at about 55 degrees to the fore and aft line of the boat, and the helm hard down. In this state *FT* apparently worked her way almost dead to windward at something between half and three-quarters of a knot. Two winters later, reading a book on trimarans, I discover that this phenomenon has been noted before. A multihull hove to under main or mizzen tends to push her bow up into the wind when a gust hits her, and very quietly, with no fuss at all, to ease her way gently straight into the wind.

On this particular day, the discovery that we have 30 miles less to go than we thought is just the tonic we need. Other things are coming right as well. The glass is continuing to rise. The wind is moving round to the North-west and is forecast to go to the West. As afternoon wears into evening, *FT* starts to put up some very fast hour's runs—9, 9½ knots—reaching towards Muckle Flugga with the wind on her beam. We are both pushing her hard now—we have a lot of time to make up. Besides, Elizabeth is coming up to meet me in Lerwick, I have not seen her for ten days, it is the longest period we have spent apart for the best part of three years since we first met. Hurry along, *FT*.

For fourteen hours, we average 9 knots, the wind continues to back and to slacken, the sea grows more leisurely. We are beginning to put the awfulness of the gale behind us, to indulge in every yachtsman's escape mechanism—to forget the wet and cold and the exhaustion, and to remember only the exhilaration, the sunlight, the fast passages. The northern lights are keeping the sky alive even at dead of night, and darkness, a sort of permanent dusk, lasts for only a little over an hour.

July 17, 5 a.m.: The 'unbreakable weld' on the bottom rudder gudgeon breaks. I am just going off watch, looking forward to some sleep. The gudgeon has parted when we are at the furthest point away from harbours and human habitation that we can possibly be on the entire Round Britain course. We are 70 miles from the Orkneys to the South-east, over 100 miles from the Isle of Lewis to the South-west and from the north coast of Scotland to the South. Muckle Flugga is 130 miles to the North-east of us, and Lerwick, the only harbour for which we have charts, is 200 miles away.

There is no question of trying to rope the rudder stock onto the transom again—we have two days of sailing ahead of us, maybe three or four, and neither of us has the stamina to hang over the transom for that long. We are carrying a spare rudder—I ordered it just in case, and it has been sitting half forgotten under the cockpit since Crosshaven, when we finally got round to attaching its gudgeons to it. We decide to fit the spare rudder, and Luke sets about dismantling the broken one.

At this point, sod's law sets in. While lifting the rudder away from the transom, Luke drops it, it floats agonisingly close by, I try and fish for it with an oar we are carrying, it is inches out of reach. Slowly, as if laughing at us, it drifts upwind, a pink patch rising and falling on a grey sea. We must retrieve it. It is a heavy object, and could cause an accident. Besides, a new one will cost £300 or £400, and the insurance will need some proof ... 'Let's attach the engine.' We argue about it for about half a minute, decide that at the most we will be penalised by the committee but not disqualified, bring up the 9 h.p. outboard engine, fit its mounting bracket, tie its safety line to a cleat, attach the petrol lead. All season, the outboard has started second or third pull. I pull it 30 times. It is dead. I find myself shouting and swearing at it, kicking the boat so hard that I bruise my toe. Luke takes over. On the fifth pull, it fires, on the tenth it is going.

We head west, steering on the motor. We have lost sight of the rudder while fighting the engine. There it is on the port bow. A small sea is running, the waves are breaking over the outboard, slamming against the wooden outboard bracket. Nearly there, we have come 300 yards, just 50 more to go. A wave hits the outboard bracket, the bracket splits in two, the outboard falls into the water, and gurgles to a halt. We haul it back on board by its safety line. There is no way we can run it again. We take one last look at the old rudder, and bid it farewell.

We haul the jury rudder up on deck—it looks alarmingly flimsy and thin. I take it aft, sit on the transom, let it down into the water intending to ease its gudgeons into the pintles so that I can drop the retaining bolts through the holes in the pintles and gudgeons to hold it in place. As I let the rudder into the water, *FT* rises gently to a wave and the rudder is almost wrenched from my hand. The short sea is sufficient to make holding a fixed rudder steady an impossible task. We both try working the bottom gudgeon into place, four hands hanging over the transom, tempting, cajoling three holes to get precisely in line with each other so that a half-inch bolt can be pushed through them. After an hour, we have still failed. We change tactics, and try and get the top gudgeon in place first. That proves fairly easy, but no sooner is it in place than the rudder blade swings and the top gudgeon cracks—the gudgeons on the spare rudder are about a quarter the strength of the rudder we have lost. For another hour, we fight to get the second gudgeon attached to the transom. After $2\frac{1}{2}$ hours, the rudder is in place, the bottom (and more important) gudgeon still in one piece, the top one split but for the moment holding together. We attach the tiller, hoist the mainsail, set a course for Muckle Flugga and start sailing again.

Luke is brutally frank about our chances. If the weather turns bad, we are in trouble. If it holds, and if the jury rudder and its pint-sized gudgeons stay in one piece, we are probably doing the safest thing to keep going for Lerwick. Since that is what I want to hear, I ask no more questions. Luke mutters something about running for shelter if the weather looks like turning bad, although where he planned to run to I have never asked.

We hoist the main with six rolls in it, and nothing else. We put down the trim board aft, and a bit of centreboard to keep as much pressure as possible off the steering. The wind is almost dead behind us. *FT* sails on at 7 knots—with the wind behind her, that appears to be as slow as she is capable of going.

I leave Luke on deck, go down below, crawl into a sleeping bag and burst into tears of frustration and paranoid rage.

July 18, 3 a.m.: We are lucky. The weather holds, we round Muckle Flugga still with only our main up, having averaged 7 knots for 19 hours. The wind is still in the West, and as we reach southwards towards Lerwick, the sun comes out and the sea flattens. We take off our oilskins for the first time for 12 days and cook some bacon and eggs. At midday, we cross the finishing line at Lerwick, just as the big red shape of *British Oxygen* is setting off for Lowestoft. Much waving and shouting across the water between us.

We tied up alongside *Quailo*—the relief that we felt was mirrored in the faces of our fellow competitors ashore. We started to hear the stories of what had happened. The gale had devastated the fleet—*Slithy Tove* broke her spreader and retired to Lerwick via the short route round the south of the island. *Croda Way* was dismasted, and back at Barra. *Minnetaree*, an Iroquois catamaran, carried away both her centreboards. A total of 14 boats were forced to retire by this gale, and many more were damaged. Most dramatic of all, *Triple Arrow*, the big, blue National Westminster Bank trimaran, had capsized within sight of the Lerwick finishing line. Brian Cooke and Eric Jensen were both all right, but the boat was in something of a mess. Out of all this, it emerged that we were still tenth, still second in our class. *Three Legs of Mann*, who missed the worst of the gale, was now over 30 hours ahead of us. At the front of the fleet, the leaders missed the gale altogether. *Three Cheers* had taken the lead, *Gulf Streamer* had moved up to second. Things had started to break on *British Oxygen*, and she had fallen back to third.

Just as I was digesting all this news, Nick Keig came aboard, looked at our jury rudder, asked us about the trip, and listened to our sad story. He casually wandered over the boat, examining it with the eye of a man who built his boat himself. He spotted something, beckoned to me. The lower starboard aluminium beam had a hairline crack in it, just short of the outrigger. I looked at the crack, which I would never have noticed myself.

Luke, Nick and I talked about it for five minutes, examined its implications. The beam of a trimaran is the most basic structural member it has, the piece that quite literally holds the whole boat together. Nick left us alone, I told Luke we were not leaving Lerwick until Derek Kelsall had seen the boat. I wandered disconsolately ashore, and almost bumped into Elizabeth in the middle of the street. Life immediately cheered up, and we both started talking at once. We found our way to a telephone booth, I phoned Derek, and he, ever generous and ever kind, promised to take the next aeroplane he could catch.

FOURTH LEG. LERWICK TO LOWESTOFT, JULY 20–23

July 20, 12.00: This is the moment at which we were supposed to be setting out across the starting line on the next leg of the course at Lowestoft. Instead, we were sitting aboard *Johnwillie*, the 46-foot trimaran that John Westell and Billy Cherry built together, sipping a drink. *Johnwillie* was one place ahead of us and should have started an hour earlier. But the BBC was forecasting a force nine westerly gale, and the Shetland fisherman who had come to join us told us that the Norwegian radio was talking about force ten. We all decided that none of us would leave until the forecast was down to force eight.

For Luke and me, there was no choice. Swarms of men with power drills had been crawling all over *FT*'s forward beam for the past 24 hours, since Derek Kelsall's arrival. An aluminium gusset plate was being fitted to the outside end of the starboard crossbeam configuration, both to take up the strains which were previously operating on the cracked section of the beam, and to beef up the whole area. The jury rudder, meanwhile, had been cased in glass fibre, and new and massively strong gudgeons had been made up for it and bolted into place. The outboard engine had been dried out and had run happily for ten hours. A new outboard bracket had been made. Luke and I had tightened every bolt holding the beams onto the boat with a ratchet spanner, and had had yet another go at some of the leaks. *FT* was to be ready in another two hours.

Poor Elizabeth had arrived in Lerwick hoping to explore the Shetland islands with me. Instead, we had never set foot outside Lerwick and she had been dragged around from one metal workshop to another She had left on the morning flight to London. It had been a harassing and tiring time, and the one consolation was that *FT* would soon be ready to sail again. The weather forecast was so awful that Luke and I could no longer bring ourselves to worry about it. Our only chance of winning this race was light airs, and quite obviously, we were not meant to win it. We would try now and hang onto second place and finish the course.

The Shetland fisherman was looking round *Johnwillie*, a beautifully finished cruising boat on which John Westell and Bill Cherry had lavished much love, and we all settled into our drinks and to talking about the gale that we should soon be sailing into. 'You are all right in a boat like this,' the fisherman declared, tapping the veneer finish round the cocktail cabinet. 'It's that boat behind you that worries me.' He was talking about *FT*. John and Bill both winked at me.

At 4 p.m., four hours after our allotted departure time, we set off from Lerwick. By the following morning, the first of a succession of gales is hitting us from just south of West. For two solid days it blows somewhere between force seven (near gale) and force eight (gale) without relenting. Every single weather forecast contains a gale warning for the area in which we are at that time sailing. As we pass eighty miles east of Wick coastal station, the shipping forecast tells us that Wick is at that very second in the teeth of a force nine (strong gale). We plug on southwards, usually with just our storm staysail up, and a heavily reefed main.

The bolts holding both the forward and aft crossbeams in place are now working loose so regularly that every second watch, one of us has to go forward into the sail locker, after four hours on watch, and spend another half hour under what amounts to a cold shower tightening the nuts with a ratchet spanner. Then the sail locker needs pumping dry—it is leaking so fast along the top crossbeam that we are carrying anything up to 40 gallons in it. Then it's back to the cockpit, where we

12 *FT* under full sail shortly after the start of the 1974 Round Britain Race. Even in this relatively smooth water she has begun to pitch to the waves. Note the fairings on the lower forward beams. (*Terry Kirk*)

13 *Quailo III*, the Admiral's Cup ocean racer and the smartest boat in the Round Britain fleet. (*Brian Manby*)

14 *Three Legs of Mann*, win
the under-35-foot class in t
1974 Round Britain Race.
Kirk) Above: Nick Keig.
(*Jeremy Greenaway*)

15 *Triple Arrow*, which cap
in the 1974 Round Britain
with Brian Cooke and Eric
aboard. On a subsequent v
Brian Cooke (above) lost h
and *Triple Arrow* was foun
capsized. (*Pickthall*)

hang upside down with water pouring up our necks, tightening more nuts. Then pump out the stern locker, then down below to pump out the main bilge, then maybe a little sleep in a sopping sleeping bag if we are lucky. Half way down the leg, having just listened to yet another gale warning on the BBC, feeling that there is no way that *FT* can ever be made ready for a trans-atlantic race, that the OSTAR project has just been a terrible mistake, I tell Luke that all I want to do is retire from the race, that if I were not sponsored, I would. Every piece of clothing we both have is wet, every leak into the cabin has opened up again. We hardly talk to each other, we scarcely eat. Just to show how terribly amusing she can be, *FT* pulls a final trick on us on the third day and the large genoa winch pulls away from the cockpit—all the bolts have sheared.

After two days and two nights of this, the gale gives up. On the third morning out, the wind has moved round to the North-east and slackened to force four, and we plane towards the Dudgeon light vessel at 9 knots. But even the weather has the last laugh on us—at midday, we arrive off Cromer with just 40 miles to go to Lowestoft and are becalmed. With nothing else to do, we turn the radio on and discover that for the last two days, Cyprus has been at war with itself.

We got into Lowestoft at 10 p.m., just in time to see *Three Legs of Mann* before she left, nearly two days ahead of us. We had discovered during the afternoon that the port forward cross-beam had cracked in exactly the same place as the starboard one did before Lerwick. Once again, our 48-hour rest period was taken up with organising boatyards and metalworkers, trying to hold *FT* together.

The saddest news to greet us in Lowestoft was that *Johnwillie* had been abandoned in mid-North Sea after one of *her* metal crossbeams had cracked in two. John Westell and Bill Cherry—both men in their 50s—had been rescued, but were said to be badly shaken. John Perry's *Peter Peter* had been dismasted, and had been towed into South Shields for repairs. *Triple Arrow*, meanwhile, had rejoined the race, and had overtaken us in the North Sea. The net result of all these alarms and excursions was that *FT* now occupied ninth place in the fleet, was still the second under-35-footer, and had a twelve-hour lead over the third boat in her class, Tony Smith's cruising trimaran *Superstar*. At the front of the fleet, the leaders had again missed the bad weather, which had allowed *British Oxygen* to re-establish a ten-hour lead over *Three Cheers*, with *Gulf Streamer* third.

FIFTH LEG. LOWESTOFT TO PLYMOUTH, JULY 25–28

We met no gales on the final leg. But once again, we were close hauled for the whole 305 miles, this time in winds of 'only' force five and six. Nothing else broke, we retained ninth place, and pulled out nearly 15 hours on *Superstar*, who finished tenth and third in our class. *Three Legs* beat us by two days and eighteen hours—a very substantial margin. Having got nine hours ahead of us at Barra, she managed to stay ahead of the worst of the dirty weather, which we made a habit of running into. More important, Nick and Peter Keig sailed a faultless race, and nothing broke on a boat that Nick had himself built. The three leaders all finished within three hours of each other, with the 70-foot *British Oxygen* holding off by a mere hour the challenge of the 46-foot *Three Cheers*. Phil Weld's big American trimaran *Gulf Streamer* was third.

ROUND BRITAIN POSTSCRIPT

The 1974 Round Britain Race was the worst single sailing experience of my life. I hated it at the time. I hate it in retrospect. I was disappointed by *FT*, and by the end of the race was in an almost permanent state of resentment and bad temper, which made me a difficult and at times impossible sailing partner. Looking back, we were lucky to reach Lerwick in one piece, and probably should not have continued racing afterwards. Nevertheless, it was a vitally important testing ground for *FT*. By the end of the race, we had shown up her weaknesses, and the fact that there were many of them, and that they were fundamental to her design and to her safety, only made it more important that we had discovered them. We had learned, too, how to sail her. We had driven her way beyond her structural limits, and close to her stability limits. From now on, all my efforts would be concentrated on making her a fast boat for shorthanded sailing, bringing out her best points, trying to by-pass or modify some of her glaring weaknesses.

From my own point of view, I had spent the summer learning what Luke thought he had forgotten. From the moment that Luke took charge when we lost our rudder off the Schelde at Easter, the relationship between us on board had been an un-stable one—he with far greater experience and a highly de-veloped instinct for what to do in an emergency; I with the ultimate responsibility for the boat, having to decide when to accept advice, when to ignore it. By the end of the Round Britain Race, the debt I owed to Luke was enormous, the lessons and experience I had gained from him a vital element in the two seasons that were to follow. During the winter, he continued to offer valuable advice on how to alter and improve *FT*. The boat that finally reached Newport in July 1976 owed more to him than he to this day realises.

Early in November, Derek, Luke and I sailed *FT* back from Chichester to Bembridge for the winter. Our final discovery before putting her to bed was that a third crossbeam had developed a crack—this time one of the aft ones, and again in exactly the same place. I left the problem in Derek's hands, and went off on a delayed honeymoon with Elizabeth—to Egypt, where we crawled in and out of 5,000-year-old tombs, and went sailing together—in a tourist Felucca at Aswan.

5

METAMORPHOSIS

January 1975: The realisation that *FT*'s beams had to be totally replaced came to me in gradual stages. I am neither an engineer nor a yacht designer, just somebody who likes to sail boats fast and safely. At the Boat Show in January, however, I began to talk to more and more people in the multihull fraternity about *FT*'s beam problems. Their almost unanimous advice: 'Ditch the metal beams—there is a fundamental weakness there, and if you strengthen one section, you will only succeed in transferring the weakness to a different point.'

There was almost unanimity, too, on what *FT* needed as a replacement—glass fibre box beams. I sought as much independent advice as I could find, and then took the train one afternoon down to Sandwich to see Derek Kelsall. He too was becoming converted to the idea of box beams for *FT*. Box beams it must be.

I had intended when I first planned this book to give a detailed analysis at this point of the changes that were made to *FT* during the 1974–75 winter. I have written it instead as an appendix, which you can either turn to now, or when you have finished reading the narrative.

By the end of January 1975, I had come to two decisions—the first was that the metal beams had to go; the second that, if this proved impossible, or if any more fundamental structural problems arose with the boat, I would withdraw from the 1976 singlehanded transatlantic race. For several nights, as I pondered these decisions, I had virtually no sleep. I had come a long way, and had put a great deal of myself into *FT*, and it was not easy to start thinking of pulling back. But I knew that to set out on the OSTAR in a boat that I did not totally trust would be gross irresponsibility. Elizabeth was now pregnant, our first child was due in the spring. The beams must be changed, or I would not go.

My next problem was to explain all this to *The Financial Times*.

Since the decision to sponsor a trimaran, the newspaper industry had moved from one of its periods of high prosperity on the back of the Heath boom into grave recession. Newsprint prices were rising rapidly, corporate advertising budgets were being cut. My decision to change the beams almost exactly coincided with *The Financial Times* 30-share index hitting a 21-year low. Because of the extensive damage of the previous summer, the trimaran project was running over budget. The OSTAR, and the publicity surrounding it, all seemed a long way away. This was not the moment to be asking for new beams.

Throughout the month of February, *FT*'s future hung in the balance. I went through a period of intense depression, convinced that the project was doomed, knowing that I had no way of financing it myself (Elizabeth had just stopped work), unable to accept that the Atlantic Race dream should come to so ignominious an end. I had vision of *FT*, unloved and unwanted, parked on the mud of some South Coast harbour, never to sail again.

I was asked by *The Financial Times* to have a study done on the proposed new beams by the Wolfson Marine Craft Unit at Southampton University. A thoroughly professional job was done by Ian Campbell of the Wolfson unit, giving the new beams a theoretical and mathematical clean bill of health—its principal conclusions are included in the appendix. Towards the end of February, I was given the go-ahead to fit the new beams, under all the circumstances a most generous decision. But it was made clear that any further major expenditures on the boat were out of the question. This was *FT*'s last chance.

Married life began rapidly to catch up with me that spring. Three weeks before our son arrived, we looked around the terraced house in which we were living in Islington and decided it was not big enough. We set out to find another house in three weeks, looked at half a dozen, and chose the one we liked most— a great Victorian pile in Clapham that would be big enough to house the large family we were planning. On the day the baby arrived, Derek Kelsall was due to deliver the new beams to Attrill's yard on the Isle of Wight. Every time I was banished from the delivery room I was on the phone to the Isle of Wight. 'I think I understand,' said the lady at Attrill's boatyard. 'You're delivering a baby with one hand, and a pair of beams with the other.' That was to be the story of my life for the next fifteen months.

In the spring of 1975, Elizabeth and I were coping with the arrival of a new baby. We were buying one house, selling another. We were trying to co-ordinate architects, builders, planners, district surveyors and the whole motley crowd who combine to make your life hell if you are silly enough to buy a house that needs conversion. At work, I was in the throes of *The Financial Times* coverage of the EEC referendum. At weekends, we were inviting parties of long-suffering friends to come and help rub down and paint *FT*.

On a Friday afternoon towards the end of May, I went down to Bembridge to conduct a test on the new beams. *FT* was suspended in mid-air from her two floats, and the centre hull was to be filled with $2\frac{1}{2}$ tons of water. Mike and Gordon Attrill both wandered round their yard with a look of dejected helplessness on their faces—they knew the test would be a disaster. I just sat there, watching *FT* slowly sag under the weight of the water, listening to the glass fibre creak and groan as she filled up, knowing that if she crashed to the floor, it was the end of both her and the OSTAR. The test had been prescribed by the Wolfson Marine Craft Unit as the final proof that the beams were up to the job, and, just as important, that they had been well and truly married to the boat.

After about three hours, the water in the main hull had reached the prescribed level. Nothing broke; nothing split; none of the bonding between the layers of glass fibre sprang. The beams were good. *FT* was in one piece again. The relief round the yard was audible.

Here, briefly, are the principal changes that had been made during the winter. The appendix contains drawings and far more detail:

1. **Beams.** A complete transplant, with the old metal beams replaced by glass fibre box beams. I hoped that these would not only prove strong enough, but would cure the problem of the leaking sail locker, since the bond between the new beams and the hull should be perfect.

2. **Rudder.** A complete redesign. The new rudder was smaller, to put less strain on its fittings, and fixed rather than lifting. A skeg was fitted under the counter to provide a third attachment point to the hull.

3. **Sail Plan.** A new forestay was fitted, and a second set of diamonds attached to the mast, to provide for a proper staysail and a really efficient cutter rig. The old no. 3 genoa, which had never been a particularly useful sail, was cut down to be a working staysail.

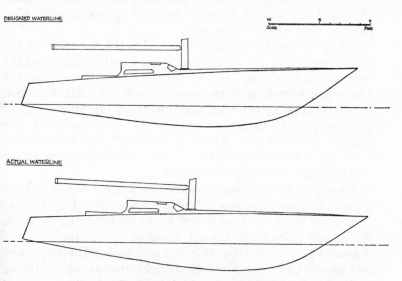

7 Designed and actual waterline.

FT's designed weight was 5,300 lb. By the time she reached the OSTAR start, she was over 30 per cent overweight, at just under 7,000 lb. The extra weight, however, was concentrated forward, so that for measurement purposes, she retained her *Jester* waterline of just under 28 feet, because her stern lifted out of the water. When the new beams were fitted during the spring of 1975, the position of the floats relative to the main hull was changed to make allowance for the way *FT* floated.

By mid-June, *FT* was back in the water, floating lower than in 1974, with the extra weight of the new beams. I took her to Cowes, where she was weighed for the multihull offshore rule measurement, and she weighed in at just under 7,000 lb—some

30 per cent. over her designed weight of 5,300 lb. Right from the word go, *FT* had floated below her designed waterline, and the distribution of her weight and buoyancy had caused her to float down at the bows. The new beams, with a heavier concentration of weight forward than aft, accentuated both these factors—at a rough guess, the new beams added some 400 or 500 lb. Ironically, the fact that *FT* floated down at the bows helped keep her within the *Jester* Trophy measurement profile. With all her stores and water out, she floated with about two feet of her transom out of the water. For her International Offshore Multihull Rule rating, her waterline was measured at 27′ 8″— just 4 inches inside the *Jester* rule.

But how would she perform when I raced her? Would the extra weight slow her down? Now that I had strengthened the beams, was I to find, like with the rudder last year, that the new and strengthened beams would transfer an additional load to another part of the boat, and something else would break? During 1974, *FT* had been on trial. In 1975, she was under suspended sentence. If she failed structurally, or if she turned out to have lost her competitive edge, she would not go to the starting line of the transatlantic race.

Three crucial races were looming up, when I would find the answers to these questions. In the first weekend in July, *FT* was entered for the Round the Island Race; the following weekend, she would defend the Crystal Trophy; at the beginning of August, I had entered the MOCRA race to Fayal in the Azores, and planned to bring *FT* back singlehanded as my qualifying cruise for the OSTAR. Elizabeth, who was badly in need of a holiday and a rest after the domestic upheavals of the previous few months, would fly out to Fayal to meet me in the middle of August. James would be left with her parents.

Yachtsmen will recognise that last paragraph as a familiar attempt to square the sailing and domestic circle. The truth about the summer of 1975 is that even without *FT*, it would have been a period of great stress and readjustment.

In the first week of July, the Government was going through the final birth pains of Stage One of its incomes policy. It was a hectic period as Fleet Street papers chased each other to be first with the definitive story on what the pay policy would be. On the Thursday, I spent most of the day driving between solicitors' and building societies' offices, finalising mortgage details, and the rest of the day and most of the night filling packing cases. On the Friday morning, we moved house—the removal van arrived at 8 a.m., and we were into our new house by about 5 p.m. The same evening, I took the last train down to Cowes. On Saturday, I raced *FT* in the Round the Island Race. On Saturday night, I was back in London. On Sunday, we tried to sort ourselves out sufficiently to camp out in the new house for the next month before going on holiday. On Monday, I was back at work, preparing for the announcement of the Government's pay policy later in the week. The following Friday, I was in Cowes again getting *FT* ready for the Crystal Trophy start on the Saturday morning. I did not return to London again until the next Wednesday.

As I write about this period now, two years later, I shudder at the strains that I was putting on my home life. I remembered ruefully a warning that Frank Page, *The Observer*'s excellent yachting correspondent, had given me two years before—very few singlehanders seem able to sustain a marriage.

6

THE AZORES

Once revamped, *FT* was quick to prove herself. In a light-weather Round the Island Race *FT* put up the fastest time of the day against a fleet of 463 boats. She also carried off all the multihull prizes. The new beams were undoubtedly heavier, but *FT* still remained the fastest light-weather boat of her size in the world. The following weekend *FT* gave an altogether pleasing performance in the Crystal Trophy, which she successfully defended. Two races in two weekends: two victories.

As I look back on the *FT* project, spanning four years of my life, leaving an indelible mark on the period, I see it as a succession of high and low points, in which the low points easily outnumbered the highs, but the highs were in a realm all of their own. The first Crystal Trophy win, the Round the Island Race, the sail back from the Azores that I shall describe later in this chapter, the 1976 *Observer* Singlehanded Transatlantic Race—these are moments in my life that I shall never forget; and the arrival in Newport was on a plane all of its own. But between all these times were months of worry and disappointment, long periods when I had trouble convincing myself that the goal I had set was worth the distance that I was having to travel to reach it.

Fayal was to be Elizabeth's holiday, the only one she would get this year. She needed a holiday badly. She would arrive in Horta, Fayal's principal town, on August 9, seven days after we set off from Portsmouth. That, I had thought, would give her a couple of days to find somewhere nice to stay, and I would arrive two or three days later. In the event, the voyage took thirteen days. Elizabeth spent six days of our holiday alone on Fayal. When I finally did arrive, there was only a week left before I had to turn round and go home again.

The feeling that the OSTAR was exacting too high a price,

that Elizabeth was being asked to sacrifice too much of her life to mine, descended on me during the race and made what should have been a pleasant if slow sail into a nightmare. I found myself tormented by feelings of guilt, and by frustration at the conflicts that my life was setting me and my inability to resolve them. Yet throughout the summer of 1975 the one option that I never seriously considered was giving up the project. My sights were set on the OSTAR, I knew what had to be done to get *FT* and myself to the starting line in a safe, seamanlike and competitive condition. Elizabeth, too, never wavered in her support for my continuing with it. What we both wanted was something that we could not have—a successful OSTAR combined with an unruffled first year of marriage.

August 2–15: The race to Fayal started off well enough. There were twelve entries, eleven of them multihulls. We set off from Portsmouth on Saturday afternoon, with a light easterly blowing up the Solent. It was the first race of its kind MOCRA had ever organised, a light-hearted, jolly affair. The starting arrangements and indeed the start itself were in the best traditions of the multihull offshore fleet—the amateur spirit much in evidence.

There were three of us aboard *FT*—Robin Musters, one of the early multihull pioneers, who now works for Tylers at Tonbridge; Robin Burroughs, who crewed on *Superstar* in the Round Britain Race; and myself. We planned to sail with one on watch at a time, and to use the trip to test all the single-handed equipment on board.

FT makes the best start, and ghosts away from the rest of the fleet towards Cowes and the Needles. As dusk falls, we are off Yarmouth, *Running Scared* is a quarter of a mile ahead of us, *Tahiti Bill* (Bill Howell) and *Triple Arrow* (Brian Cooke) are within sight of us behind. As usual in light airs, *FT* is among boats far larger than herself.

Running Scared is obviously going to be the boat to beat. She was built last winter for a Swedish architect and his wife; her Australian designer, Lock Crowther, is a member of the crew; so are some of the best seamen among the MOCRA membership, notably David Walsh. *Running Scared* has shown herself in the Crystal Trophy race to be faster than *FT* to windward, and now she is going faster than us under spinnaker.

For the first two and a half days, we never down our spinnaker, as we cream out into the Western Approaches in a freshening easterly. Then, in the middle of the second night, Robin Musters comes off watch, and Robin Burroughs takes over in the cockpit. I have been woken up twice in the last hour by the sound of a spinnaker flogging as *FT* broached and Robin Musters fought her back on course. Musters and I have a brief discussion on whether to take the big spinnaker down. But before it is over, the decision has been taken for us—Robin Burroughs, fresh on watch, taking time to get used to the motion of the boat and the sea, loses her, she broaches, there is a sudden torrent of swearing from on deck, and I rush up to find the spinnaker in shreds, flapping wildly, totally out of control.

In one sense, we are lucky—the tapes that are sewn along each edge of the spinnaker have held, so that although the chute itself is in five pieces, the outside edges have all stayed together. It takes us about fifteen minutes to get it down. Only then do I realise that we have been carrying a 1200-square-foot light-weather spinnaker in force six to seven. With *FT* surging at up to 14 knots, however, we have not felt the strength of the breeze. We are lucky to have got off as lightly as we have. If one of the tapes had gone, the sail would now be wrapped around the forestay, and one of us would have to climb the mast to wrestle with it, probably for many hours.

Almost as soon as the spinnaker is under control, the weather changes, making a commentary all of its own on our stupidity in holding onto the big sail. The wind now goes dead light, we are at the centre of a complex of electric storms which are lighting up the sky all around us, sending great rolls of thunder to shatter the night. Before dawn a southerly comes in and we are off again, under no. 2 genoa and reefed main, averaging a steady 8 knots.

Shortly after dawn, *Croda Way* appears on the horizon; Mike Best, a burly 46-year-old army captain with a large handlebar moustache, has on board his student daughter Patricia and the company pilot from Croda International, which sponsors the boat. *Croda Way* is a 35-foot Simpson-Wilde trimaran with a

33-foot waterline, too large for the *Jester* trophy in the OSTAR, probably too small to win the *Gipsy Moth* intermediate class. Nonetheless, Mike is determined to do the transatlantic and is using the Fayal race in the same way as I am—he too will sail back alone. *FT* and *Croda Way* have had several close races together, notably the first leg of the Round Britain when they finished a minute apart. Now, here they were together again, after 250 miles of sailing.

People on land never really understand the vast size of the sea. The chances of two boats, even two boats going to and from the same place, meeting up in mid-ocean are tiny—visibility at sea is only a few miles, and the action of the wind, different boat speeds and different tactical decisions by skippers normally keep yachts out of sight of each other. During the whole of the transatlantic race, when 125 boats went to the starting line, I never sighted another competitor after the first twenty-four hours.

But today, here is *Croda Way*, half a mile away. All day, we remain within sight of each other. As night comes in, we continue to watch *Croda Way*'s lights. The following morning, she is still with us—for twenty-four hours we have travelled at exactly the same speed. Then, as the wind gradually begins to increase and to head us on the morning of August 5, *FT* starts falling into her bad habits. She begins to buck, and even without her bottom forward beam, she still slams hard into the sea with her somewhat bulbous underwater shape. *Croda Way*, with her extra length on the waterline, is soon over the horizon and away.

All that morning, we are reducing sail, first to our cutter rig with the yankee jib up, then to staysail and heavily reefed main. Soon after breakfast, I try doing a turn sewing the spinnaker and am promptly sick. At mid-day, I am woken by the high-pitched whine of a new wind speed alarm I have fitted during the winter, and leap out of my bunk to find that we are in the middle of a nasty storm. Within seconds of getting up, a squall hits us, visibility is down to 40 yards, the wind speed alarm hovers around 45 knots as we pound forward into the sea. 'Take the staysail down, we're heaving to.' Within a minute, the motion of the boat is suddenly peaceful. *FT* has stopped moving. Outside, the squall has flattened the sea, everything is white, spray is being picked up by the wind and driven horizontally across the water, the wind is squealing through the rigging and we have to shout to make ourselves heard. But *FT*, with her mainsail rolled almost right down, and her helm hard over, is perfectly comfortable. She rises and falls to the seas life a raft, just as she had the previous summer between St Kilda and Muckle Flugga. We all go to sleep, and leave the gale to rage around us.

What a change from last season, when the whole idea of heaving to was anathema to me. A year and a half's experience has taught me a lot. I know that to push *FT* on through the gale will put great strains on her and on us; I know that even if we keep going at an average of 3 to 4 knots, our real distance made good will be small, and certainly not worth the risks. We are the only boat in the fleet to take this action, and some of those who do not pay heavily for it—*Croda Way* keeps going, but the effort so exhausts her crew that it is two days before they have really recovered; *Tahiti Bill*, the eight-year-old Rudy Choy-designed catamaran that Bill Howell has already sailed in two transatlantic races and will enter for a third time next year, breaks both her centreboards, and continues towards Fayal without them. It is an important lesson which I carry through to the OSTAR—don't strain the boat unnecessarily.

At the point that the gale hits us, about midday on August 5, we have made tremendous progress—440 miles or about a third of the course in less than three days. The atmosphere on board has been jovial and optimistic. Now, we enter a four-day period when our average daily run sinks to 75 miles. For the first two, I am continuously seasick, unable to hold down food, realising that my strength and even my will are slowly disappearing.

Seasickness is a strange illness. If you allow it to get on top of you, then quickly you lose all energy, all will to do anything. I have seen strong and healthy men reduced to a useless corpse within an hour of its onset. The only way to fight it is to ignore it, just to keep on doing what you have to do, and wait for your body to overcome it. It is so long since I have been seasick that having to face up to it again after so many years is a severe blow—just ten months before the OSTAR start. One of the secrets is not to try and do too much while you are ill—

straining your body or your mind just makes it worse again. Thus, I find that although I can take sunsights, looking up the figures and trying to order my mind enough to work them out is too much—I am promptly ill again. If I do anything strenuous on deck—pumping out the bilges, unwrapping a vagrant flag halyard which has bound itself into a tight knot round the cap shroud—my stomach heaves fifteen minutes later. There is nothing in it any more—Bovril and dried biscuits are all I have been asking it to take, and it holds on to those for just as long as I do nothing mentally or physically strenuous.

But the other feature of seasickness is that recovery is almost instantaneous. I saw a man once—after fourteen hours totally prostrate, unable even to move from one bunk to another without being carried—start eating a fried chicken leg within fifteen minutes of our return to calm water. On this sail, I slowly recover, under the wise guidance of Robin Musters (both Robins had been ill on the Crystal; neither is on this trip). But in order to recover and keep the boat going, I leave all the heavy work to them, and do no navigating. Supposing this had been the OSTAR? Then what?

August 8: Tomorrow, Elizabeth arrives in Fayal. For two days, the wind has been dead ahead of us and light. Now it leaves us entirely. There are still 700 miles to go to Horta. The sun is beating down, not a ripple on the sea. We all strip off and swim. But my mood is beginning to permeate the boat. It is a tiny space in which the three of us are confined, and as I sink into gloom and depression, the two Robins valiantly try and lift me out of it.

Elizabeth had been dubious about the holiday from the start. Long before we married, it was clear that she was never going to be what she calls 'a hearty lady'. Gentle sails on smooth water with the sun out, occasional one-day passages with a good, preferably French meal at the end of them—that was where she wanted sailing to end, and she was happy to let me pursue it beyond that point on my own. She had asked for and I had promised her a real holiday together. Now, as I sit contemplating the flat sea around me, that holiday is slipping away.

I start measuring off distances on the chart—it is only 325

miles to Northern Spain, perhaps we should go there, and Elizabeth could fly to Lisbon and take the train up ... the logistics are daunting, and we put off a decision until the next day to see if an honest wind arrives. All that night, we just slop, with our sails down. The following morning, a force four arrives from the South, and we decide that that is honest enough and head for Horta.

It is another week before we arrive. A week of more calms, more gloom from the skipper. For one glorious 24-hour stretch, the wind pipes up from the North, we carry our no. 2 spinnaker throughout (the two Robins are still sewing the no. 1), and do 207 miles from midday sunsight to midday sunsight—the only 200-mile day I shall ever do in *FT*. But the high spirits generated by that burst of speed are quickly lost again in more days of calms.

The end of the race is full of ironies. On the morning of August 14, we find ourselves 10 miles north of Terceira. Robin Burroughs, an army captain, is supposed to be picking up a military flight that is due to land at Terceira that day. We have about an hour's debate before deciding that since we must have lost the race, since Robin needs to get home, since I want to get a message to Elizabeth that we are all right, we will motor into Terceira, drop Robin off, and Robin Musters and I will complete the race on our own. We motor towards Terceira (allowed under the rules provided you go back to the point where you started motoring before sailing again), and find a little cove where we anchor. Robin Burroughs and I row ashore and almost immediately bump into the village policeman, who has some trouble understanding what two foreigners who speak not a word of his language are doing scrambling ashore on a piece of lonely coastline from a funny-looking pink boat. He decides to keep an eye on us, and accompanies us to the nearest shop, where we make a phone call to Horta, get a message to Elizabeth, and learn that *Triple Arrow* and *Running Scared* have arrived—no one else. *Running Scared* has therefore beaten us, whatever we do. We order a taxi.

Three hours later, still with the policeman in tow, I have dropped Robin off at the US Air Force base; filled up with stores from the local American PX (we have been on rationing for the last four days); changed some money with a backstairs moneychanger (the banks are all shut, but the policeman quickly leads us to the black market); and am back on board again. Robin Musters and I motor back to the point we first started from, and rejoin the race.

We arrive in Horta the following afternoon after one of the most glorious and beautiful day's sailing of my life, past the green slopes of São Jorge; round the rocky headland of Ponta dos Rosais to our first view of Pico, a great green volcanic peak that rises 7,700 feet above the water; up to the shores of Pico and through the Canal do Faial, with Pico almost leaning over us; sun out, wind rising all day, warm spray breaking over the boat. In the Canal do Faial, it starts to gust up to over 30 knots, and we are down to our cutter rig. Just before the finish, we relax, and sail right in under the cliffs, almost onto the rocks. It is a foolish and thoroughly unseamanlike thing to do, the wind dies, we almost miss a tack, for five awful seconds I realise that if she does not come round, we must end up on the rocks. She does come round. We are at the finish. Elizabeth is there in a little runabout, waving, smiling bravely. As we enter Horta, fireworks start exploding around us, the whole town seems to be alight.

The following morning, we were disqualified for dropping off Robin Burroughs (we had expected a time penalty, but knew that disqualification was a possibility). I learnt that at the time we decided to motor to Terceira, after twelve days at sea, we were within five miles of three other boats—*Croda Way*, *Tahiti Bill* and *Gipsy Moth* (sailed by the late Sir Francis Chichester's son Giles). If we had not dropped out we would have had a splendid race through the islands with all three of them for third place home. Perhaps more important, when David Walsh settled down to analyse the race, he found that three days from the finish, *FT* was actually leading the fleet—ahead both of *Triple Arrow* and *Running Scared*—before we ran into yet another wind hole while they carried their wind with them. It was this information, coupled with *FT*'s displays in the Round the Island and Crystal Trophy, that finally persuaded me not to reduce the size of *FT*'s long mast and large sail plan for the OSTAR.

She was so fast in light weather that I dared not risk losing her light-weather speed for uncertain gain in stronger winds. My strategy for the OSTAR from this point on firmed: I would sail to *FT*'s strengths, go for the light weather. That meant taking the southern route.

By now, I knew I had a fast boat. I was pretty sure that I had a strong and seaworthy boat. There was one question left that I had still to resolve—how would I react when alone at sea? The OSTAR rules require a 500-mile qualifying cruise. I had gone to the Azores, and dragged Elizabeth there with me, so that my qualifying cruise would be a really long one, and I would discover whatever there was to learn about how I react to myself.

Sunday, August 24: Mid-afternoon and I am on my way. The sun is out, the wind is blowing from the South, the weather charts indicate that I should have steady, following winds the whole way home. I fantasise on reaching Plymouth in seven or eight days.

My first reaction to being alone is all the more curious for being totally unexpected. For years now—ever since a close friend was drowned 15 yards from a rescue boat—I have always sailed wearing a lifejacket. Now, within the first hour of leaving Horta, I twice find myself looking at the lifejacket hanging in the oily locker and rejecting it. There is no thought behind this decision. It is a purely subconscious acceptance of the worst risk I face singlehanded—that of falling overboard. When *FT* is moving, she is usually going at a minimum of 6 knots. If she and I part company, her self-steering will keep her going, and there is no way in the world that I will ever get back to her. A lifejacket will not make the slightest difference. It would merely prolong the agony as she sailed herself away over the horizon.

As dusk falls on the first night, I am heading north-east under spinnaker, with the lights of Graciosa, the northernmost Azorian island, on my starboard beam. The Tillermaster electric self-steering system, which served us well on the way out, is keeping an accurate compass course, the wind is steady, and I decide to go to sleep leaving the spinnaker up. During the winter months, sitting in my study at home trying to think things through, I had decided that I could never do this—the risk of a sudden wind change, of waking up to a spinnaker in total control of the boat would be too high. Now, on my first substantial singlehanded sail, it seems the most natural thing to do in the world—the night is so calm and peaceful, the boat so steady.

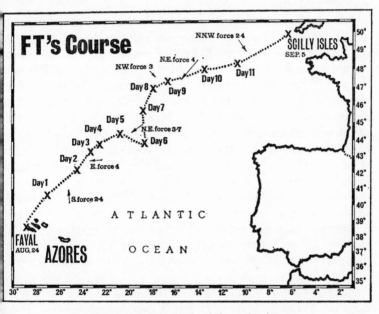

FT's Course

NNW force 2-4

SCILLY ISLES
SEP. 5

N.E. force 4

N.W. force 3

Day 10   Day 11

Day 8   Day 9

Day 7

Day 5

Day 4

N.E. force 3-7

Day 3

Day 6

Day 2

E. force 4

Day 1

S. force 2-4

ATLANTIC

FAYAL
AUG. 24   **AZORES**

OCEAN

8 *FT*'s course on route back from the Azores.

I set my two alarm clocks for one hour's sleep, lead the spinnaker sheet to within a few inches of my head so that in an emergency I can let it go quickly and collapse the spinnaker, and put my head down. I hear neither of the two alarm clocks when they go off. Instead, I wake several hours later with a start, and instinctively let the sheet go. Something is different, what is it? I am out of my sleeping bag and up on deck in one movement, trying to sort out what has happened. The night is still a bright one, the stars are still out, the spinnaker is still drawing. But *FT* is moving at $9\frac{1}{2}$ knots; of course, the wind has increased in strength, while I have been asleep we have doubled our speed. I sit on the edge of the cockpit, and watch *FT* gliding gracefully over the water. It is blowing at about 15 knots, force four. The sea is still calm. The self steering is keeping her on course. *FT* is in one of her happiest moods. I stay up on deck for five minutes, watch her through a couple of gusts, and then, slightly to my own surprise, go down below again, set the alarms, and go back to sleep.

For two days it is like this—steady but non-violent following winds. In that time, I have done 300 miles, and write smugly in my log—'it took four days to finish from this point.' After three days, I have done 400 miles, a third of the way home. But now the first things begin to go wrong. The electric self-steering gives up the ghost, I spend many hours playing with it, trying to entice it back into life—all fail. More seriously, I find one of my two batteries is dead after twenty-four hours. I was worried about it in Horta, but the man who recharged it for me swore it was all right. The plunger in my thirty-year-old hurricane lamp turns out to be rotten, and it falls to bits in my hand—I can no longer pump pressure into it. That will make me less visible at night, which worries me a little, especially as the one battery I have left may not power my masthead navigation lights all the way home, I have no generator on board, one of the solar cell generators is not working, and the other is working only fitfully.

But the loss of the Tillermaster turns out to be a blessing in disguise. Whether I like it or not, I now *have* to use the Hasler wind vane, even for downwind work. Over the rest of this voyage, I learn more about balancing *FT* with a sheet adjustment here, a touch of the centreboard there, than I had learned in the whole of the previous two seasons. I find to my surprise that in almost every kind of wind, *FT* and the Hasler between them can be made to steer *some* sort of more or less straight course in more or less the direction I am trying to go.

The galloping start I have made over the first three days is too good to last. The fourth day is one of calms, when I move only 30 miles; on the fifth a weather system passes through, bringing with it a day of constantly changing wind strengths and directions. I spend almost all day on deck, changing sails, altering course, getting nowhere, exhausting myself. By now I am within range of BBC shipping forecasts again, and the first one I hear is talking about north-easterlies.

North-easterlies. That is dead against me. The weather chart tells me I have a seventy per cent. chance of westerly winds, which is just what I want, and only a five per cent. chance of north-easterlies. But north-easterlies it is to be, almost non-stop for the next week. Just to whet my appetite, the wind comes in at force six on the sixth day, and rises through the night to force seven (near gale), bringing with it a confused and breaking sea. During the night, the noise becomes altogether too much for me, and I heave to for four hours and snatch some good sleep. The sleep drives some sense into me. I have spent 24 hours on port tack—'the making tack' for the Scillies, which has been taking me west towards Northern Spain. I should be pushing north, making for the westerlies and south-westerlies in the Western Approaches. Moral—on long passages, think strategy not tactics. Strategy demands that I should be heading north not west. Only the shortest-term tactical considerations caused me to make this silly tack, that has wasted at least a day.

Four hundred miles over the first three days; 240 over the next four. Not very good.

But now, after a week at sea, I take careful stock of what is happening to me. The first and most pleasing discovery is that I am thoroughly enjoying myself. Far from being frightened by being alone at sea, I have been exhilarated. After the strains of the sail down, the worries over Elizabeth and her holiday, I have found a deep sense of peace during the first week at sea. Loneliness? 'It is hardly affecting me at all,' I write in my log. 'There just seems to be so much to keep me busy—a boat to sail and navigate, a person to feed and look after, a constantly expanding list of little jobs that need doing around *FT*. My biggest problem is to convince myself that I am alone at all, especially when I wake up in the night. In that half-awake, half-asleep state of semi-consciousness, I have found myself happily believing that someone else is sailing the boat. There are all the familiar noises—sea gurgling past the hull, wind whistling through the rigging, *FT* crashing through waves. My half-conscious brain associates those noises with Luke or one of the Robins being on deck. Twice, I have just fallen back to sleep again.

'With no one to talk to and no one to bounce decisions off, I keep a constant dialogue going with myself, talking out loud. I have practically created two people out of myself, and am amused to find on reflection that these two people conform to two distinct strains in my personality. On the one hand is the bit of me that always wants to do things two minutes before I first thought of them, which puts up all the suggestions, is constantly urging action. On the other is an altogether more circumspect individual, who likes to weigh up decisions before acting on them, and is for ever playing devil's advocate to the first.

'Early in the sail, the first of these two personae was very much in the ascendant. At night, the alarm clock was set every hour, sails kept being changed, jobs were done as if the boat's life depended on their completion, sheets were never left unadjusted for more than 10 minutes. After two days, I was totally exhausted. Now, the second persona is in the ascendant. I am taking six, seven, even eight hour sleeps, without setting the alarm at all, relying on the boat to wake me up if something changes. Two nights ago, I woke at precisely the moment the self-steering was inadvertently putting the boat about. "The boat is about to come to a standstill. Wake up, get up and go and put her back on course," I told myself firmly. "Go to hell," myself replied from the very depths of a warm sleeping bag, "it's 2.30 a.m. and no time for that sort of thing." It was two hours before the two of us woke up again, two hours during which we could have been sailing 12 miles and instead remained stationary.'

My log on this day is flooded with optimism; the person writing it appears to have been more relaxed than at any stage since *FT* first went into the water. The sea, the great Atlantic ocean that I am sailing alone for the first time in my life, is being kind to me, is putting on a gala performance, feasting me with a full moon for almost all the first week, three stunning sunsets, relaxing weather.

It is during that first week that I am standing on the boat's counter, trying to get the hurricane lamp to work. My log takes up the story: 'It is 2 a.m., a bright starlit night, the moon almost full. As I wrestle with the lamp, I suddenly hear a long and very loud snort, followed by an equally long exhaustive noise, something half way between a sigh and a wheeze. I find myself clutching the backstay, then cautiously returning to the cockpit —on tiptoes of all things. Then I hear the noise again, from the direction of the moon. I look along the shimmering surface of the water to see, silhouetted against the moonlight, the back of a huge whale. It rises to the surface, has a brief look at me, then dives back again into 15,000 feet of endless ocean. Will it come back? Will it touch the boat? I feel terribly small, the boat seems so frail. Just one touch from that great fluke, and *FT* will be shattered. But the leviathan is gone, leaving behind the memory of a sight at once awesome and beautiful, which will be with me for the rest of my life.'

All this is in my log for August 31, during my eighth day at sea, when the wind is beginning to veer towards the east, blowing a gentle force three–four, and I am pointing at about 40 degrees Magnetic, near enough to the right direction to make me feel I am getting somewhere.

Just 24 hours later, a quite different mood has taken hold: 'No wind since midnight. All day, I have sat lolling in the ocean with the sails down, searching the sky for any sign of wind. Intense depression is setting in. I am trying to fight off, with no success at all, waves of self-pity and paranoia. I am going to be late, Elizabeth will start worrying about me, I cannot get in touch with her. I have done all the jobs I can possibly do, and there is nothing else to do, no decisions to take. I cannot even relax enough to read.' It is my first encounter with the singlehander's greatest mental enemy—a flat calm.

A day later, the wind is back, and so are my good spirits. 'Just after my midday sunsight, I pass a ship, just half a mile away. The big genny is up, we are on a close reach dead on course for the Bishop, travelling at over 7 knots. I wave to the ship, watch through the binoculars the tiny figures on the bridge who are in turning looking at *FT* through their binoculars. The ship passes, and I decide to go out to the lee float to fiddle around with something. I am standing on the lee float, half concentrating on the job I am doing, half watching the ship chugging on towards the horizon when I lose my balance and find myself falling backwards. I grasp at a sheet—it is not belayed. I grab the spinnaker sheet, take up about six inches of slack and find myself hanging over the water, almost in it. I am attached by a long lifeline. But I have often wondered what would actually happen if *FT* started dragging me through the water at 7 knots. How easy would it be to get back on board? Would I swallow water, be pulled under? I have no wish to find out. It was an idiotic mistake, caused by overconfidence, the feeling that because a boat was nearby, I was no longer alone. I go back to the cockpit, cursing myself, my legs shaking.'

On September 5, after a little over 12 days at sea, I make it to the Scillies. I drift in on the very faintest of zephyrs, with no charts, only Adlard Coles's splendid little *Guide to South Coast Harbours* to help me find my way. The relief at arriving is intense. My batteries are almost dead. I am very tired. The wind is dying. If I had not made the Scillies tonight, I would have faced a night in the shipping lanes with no navigation lights, no motor, no wind, and probably unable to stay awake. I can imagine few situations more dangerous. Once before, on the only previous singlehanded sail I have done, I allowed myself to become exhausted when close to land. I became so tired that my brain literally stopped functioning. It happened at dawn, after I had been up all night. I found myself a mile from the Lizard, and totally becalmed. Suddenly, I noticed a model ship passing me just a few yards away; then another; then what looked like a model of the *Mayflower*. Funny, I thought to myself, there must be a model ship rally out of Falmouth. Then, for a few brief seconds, my eyes focused properly on the ships. They turned out to be full size, two or three miles away, and the *Mayflower* was indeed a replica, with full sails up. Within seconds, my eyes were again sending false messages to my exhausted brain, and I was again seeing models. I was so tired I could not even persuade myself to put the anchor down. I just hove to and collapsed. Three hours later, I woke to find myself 200 yards from the Lizard rocks.

Tonight, as I put my anchor down in St Mary's and dusk falls, my relief at arriving is total. I have qualified for the

OSTAR. I have thoroughly enjoyed the sail. Except for the boat's electrics, which will need totally renewing during the winter, everything has worked—or almost everything, anyway.

7

FINAL PREPARATIONS

In one sense, the sail back from the Azores was too successful. The boat had performed so well, I had learned so much, that I relaxed a little, began to feel that my problems were over. 'A sail like that gives you tremendous confidence, doesn't it,' said Brian Cooke as we chatted over the telephone one day. It certainly had. After so much worry, after so many things had gone wrong, it all seemed to be coming together.

It was now that I started to train. At first, runs round Clapham Common, one or two games of squash a week, then a slow build-up at Al Murray's City gymnasium under the BP Building during the lunch hour whenever I found time to get there. I stopped smoking in January; cut out all forms of working lunches in April (mainly to make time to visit the gym or to do the continuous round of visits to chandlery shops); gave up drinking in May (well almost—wine is all that I ever drink, and just the odd glass here and there may have got past the censor).

Down at Bembridge, the Attrills were doing their usual superb job on *FT*. As always happens with them, she went into the water on precisely the day they had said she would—March 5. For the next month, Rupert Lyle, a young man in his early twenties with a passion for boats, worked on her every day, going through a long list of items that I had drawn up the previous summer—little details that make all the difference when you are alone at sea. Rupert was to labour on *FT* for most of the spring. For the final two weeks before the OSTAR, he lived on board in Plymouth, looking after every tiny detail. He more than anyone else is responsible for the fact that *FT* set off from Plymouth as well prepared as any boat in the fleet.

Meanwhile in London, I was working on strategy, trying to think through every possible situation that I might meet, and to make sure I was prepared for it.

Most OSTAR competitors think in terms of two routes—the 'northern' or 'Great Circle' route and the 'southern' or 'Azores' route. The Azores route had been pioneered in the 1968 race by an American yacht skipper and deliverer called Tom Follett. He had arrived at Plymouth in a 40-foot Atlantic Proa called *Cheers* designed by an unknown Virgin Islander, Dick Newick, and had almost not been allowed to enter. *Cheers* went south and finished third in the then very fast time of 27 days. Two days before the finish, she was leading, but sailed into a calm patch.

Then in 1972, many more entries followed the *Cheers* trail. *Cap 33*, a large French trimaran, finished third in just over 24 days; *Toucan*, Alain Gliksman's long, slim lake-sailor, won the under 35-foot class in $28\frac{1}{2}$ days on the Azores route. Six of the first ten finishers went south, and seven of the first fourteen. If I had any remaining doubts about the route, Nick Keig in *Three Legs of Mann* resolved them for me. In the 1975 AZAB singlehanded race, he covered the distance from Falmouth to São Miguel in just seven days. Even allowing for the fact that *FT* was not as fast an allround boat as *Three Legs*, I reckoned I would have covered the distance in a maximum of eight days in the same conditions—and after that, I would be over a third of the way to Newport.

The southern route is the light-air route, taking you south of the contrary Gulf Stream, and it is the warm route. Its great disadvantage is that it is theoretically 450 miles longer than the Great Circle—roughly 3,300 miles against 2,850. The justification for taking it is that the prevailing winds are more favourable, and that therefore the distance sailed *through the water* may be less than the boats who go north and have to beat all the way. *Cheers* actually sailed less miles than the two boats that beat her in 1968.

For *FT* and me, the southern route almost chose itself. At the time she went to the start at Plymouth, she was the fastest light-weather boat of her size in the world. In a sea, even after changing her beams, she was still frankly a bitch. I had to sail to her strength, and gamble against running out of wind entirely—the main danger of the southern route is that you get caught in the Azores High-pressure system and spend days

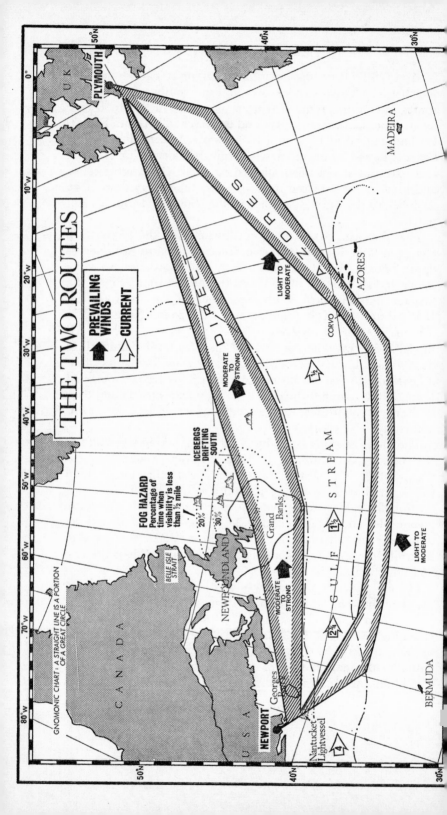

getting nowhere. The northern route was not even an option—
FT was not a heavy weather boat, she was not in anything above
moderate airs a windward boat, and I was not at all sure how
she would ride out a really severe north Atlantic storm.

Then there was my own preference. I had discovered during
the Round Britain Race that I am not one of life's masochists.
Wet, cold and seasick is not a formula to keep my morale up
or my efficiency high. *FT* is a wet boat, she requires constant
sail changes to keep her going at her best. The sea that would
be breaking over me on the northern route would be very cold
indeed, and colder still as I entered the fog and iceberg zone
around the Grand Banks of Newfoundland.

The icebergs, too, played an important part in my thinking.
At some point as you plan an attack on the OSTAR, you have
to take a decision on the size of risk you are prepared to take to
win the race. I had read of previous competitors sniffing out
icebergs with their water thermometer, in conditions where
they could see nothing because of darkness or fog or both. That
was too high a risk to take. And as I found myself saying that,
I added something else—my order of priorities for this race
would be: stay alive, get there, win. No false heroics.

◀ 9 'The two routes'.
The two principal routes, divided by the Gulf Stream. Even to the North of
the warm Gulf Stream waters, there is an adverse current averaging about
half a knot. But once on the Grand Banks, the direct-route boats start to pick
up the South-flowing Labrador current. A few competitors have tried more
extreme routes in the OSTAR. In 1968, Michael Richey took *Jester* down
to the Trade Winds around 25 degrees South. He was the last to finish, in 57½
days, and the route has not been tried since. A more plausible route for
serious racers is the far northern route, which Blondie Hasler successfully
pioneered in the first race of all. Mike McMullen often talked of taking
Three Cheers on this route—his plan was to sail a Great Circle course to the
Belle Isle Strait and then round the back of Newfoundland. The advantage
of doing this is that the prevailing winds tend to be more from the South
than from the West at about 55 degrees North. The disadvantages are that
it adds distance (about 170 miles extra was McMullen's calculation for his
Belle Isle Strait course); and you are likely to be nearer the centres of the
lows, and therefore in even worse weather than on the direct route. We have
no means of knowing which route McMullen took. But if he took the far
northern route, he could well have been near the centre of both the third
(June 12) and the fourth (June 14) gales.

So the decision was taken. I would go south. I felt sure that I would beat any boat of my own size who came south with me. I therefore decided to publicise my decision as much as possible, and in articles in both *The Financial Times* and *Yachts and Yachting*, sang the praises of light airs and warm seas.

I decided to set a target for myself. *Toucan* had won the under 35-foot class in $28\frac{1}{2}$ days in 1972, which was thought to be a remarkable time. But in 1972, there had been no waterline-length restriction, so that *Toucan* had been considerably longer in this all-important department than the 1976 *Jester* class would be. Somewhat arbitrarily, I concluded that 28 days would win me the *Jester* Trophy, and that I would use this as a benchmark on the way across. Twenty-eight days would also ensure that I reached America the day before the July 4 celebrations, so there was a double incentive.

I decided that I would not steer the boat, but would cross on self-steering. Partly this was because I had sailed like this on my way back from the Azores, and *FT* had gone well; partly, it was to try and keep me from becoming overexhausted. I knew that steering the boat a lot would mean being almost continuously wet. I felt that winning the transatlantic was not about going at maximum efficiency some of the time; it was about going at reasonable efficiency all of the time. Above all, it was about not making serious errors, about staying alert. One bad navigational error because I was tired, I argued to myself, would cost me more than I would ever gain by steering the boat every day.

One weekend in early February, Elizabeth and I took James down to Devon to spend the weekend with my father. I had all my charts with me, and spent much of Saturday—or as much as James would allow—plotting positions, trying to work out who had gone where and why during the 1972 race, and marking some of the leaders' positions on my two principal working charts.

On the Sunday morning, the papers told me what I had feared for about a month—that Brian Cooke's trimaran *Triple Arrow* had been found upside down, with no sign of life on board and the liferaft still attached. Brian was dead. His death hit everybody who had known Brian. It also brought home to those of us who were planning to take part in the race just what we were doing. A few months before, it was Brian who had said to me on the telephone after my sail back from the Azores: 'A sail like that gives you tremendous confidence, doesn't it.' He had had confidence in *Triple Arrow*.

I spent a week unable to sleep. Elizabeth was magnificent, helping me regain my nerve. I discovered everything I could about Brian's death—the evidence was sketchy, but pointed to his having fallen overboard, with *Triple Arrow* subsequently capsizing. Slowly, I drove away the anxieties and fears his death had brought. By the end of February, I was feeling reasonably confident again, looking forward to *FT*'s launch in early March. The previous winter, in the middle of *FT*'s beams crisis, one of the directors of *The Financial Times* had taken me to one side and warned: 'The hardest thing of all that you may have to accept is a loss of nerve at the last minute. Even at that late stage, you may have to admit to yourself that you cannot go.' It was a generous and understanding thing to say, and a tremendous relief to hear it from my employer and sponsor.

But by the end of February, I was already past the point of turning back. Perhaps Brian Cooke's death was that point. My reaction to it was to refuse to allow the thought of turning back to enter my mind. As I assimilated the news, I was finding ways of driving out fears and doubts. Pride and self-respect and the knowledge that if I did turn back, I would regret it all my life, all required me to appear at the starting line at Plymouth.

I had only one more serious attack of pre-race nerves. That was in May, during my last week at work, when I heard of yet another trimaran accident, this one happily not fatal. Phil Weld, with one crew on board, capsized the 60-foot *Gulf Streamer* while sailing her over for the race. We had all assumed that *Gulf Streamer*—a light-displacement boat with a low aspect rig—was uncapsizeable. We had all been wrong. Phil Weld and his crew lived on board for several days in the warm Gulf Stream waters before being rescued, but the boat was left in mid-Atlantic. Again, I found out as much as I could about the accident, and tried to work out how and why it had happened. I tore out of the newspaper the story that reported it, so that Elizabeth would not see it, and I never told her about it.

I had planned to spend almost every weekend in April and May practising, but the weather let me down. I went to Cherbourg for Easter, loaded up with French canned food for the voyage. But on three successive weekends in April and early May, there was too little wind to justify taking *FT* out sailing. Instead, I returned to London to spend the weekend with Elizabeth and James. Partly it was that I knew I was going to be away from James for a long time, and I wanted to see as much of him as possible—he was now one, and just starting to walk. Partly it was that I was still basking in overconfidence from the sail back from the Azores—it had gone so well that I now felt that as long as I had one good heavy weather bash before the race to make sure nothing would break, that was all I and the boat needed.

We had such a bash three weekends before the start. I entered the Crystal Trophy, which attracted an even smaller and poorer entry than in 1975. It blew a nasty force seven to eight for most of the first day, *FT* went very slowly, and I was very seasick. Just after dark on the second evening, we listened to a shipping forecast of another westerly gale during the night, and we retired into Plymouth rather than risk damage to the boat, or more discomfort for a weakening skipper.

On a Friday afternoon, eight days before the OSTAR, I at last got into the front of our Mini, its back loaded with gear, and set off for the M4. I found saying goodbye to James unbearably painful. I knew that I might not see him again, that if I did not, I would just be a picture on his wall as he grew up. Leaving him standing gurgling in his playpen was the worst single moment of this whole venture.

Down in Plymouth, the OSTAR jamboree was cranking into gear. Millbay Dock was filling up with every conceivable size and shape of boat. Would we pass our inspection? Would *FT* be judged within the *Jester* profile? We did and she was. I was tense and anxious, but I noticed signs of even more tension and anxiety around me, particularly among the heavily sponsored skippers.

The three people in particular who caught my attention, for entirely different reasons, were Eric Tabarly, Alain Colas and Michael Kane. Tabarly was moored just behind me in Millbay.

16 The two Dick Newick designed trimarans, *Three Cheers* and *Gulf Streamer*, close reaching at speed. Both boats were lost during the summer of 1976. This photograph had a substantial impact on our thinking for *FT*'s revised sail plan. Note the very low aspect rigs, and the positioning of the staysail. (*Beken*) Insets: Mike McMullen, Phil Weld. (*Multihull International*)

17 *FT* makes her late start away from the *Jester* line. Fifty yards ahead of her is *Spaniel*. (*Glyn Genin*)

18 Even the 62-foot trimaran *Spirit of America* (Michael Kane) is dwarfed by the 236 feet of Alain Colas's monster *Club Méditerranée* as they cross the OSTAR starting line. (*Ashley Ashwood*)

He arrived with what appeared to be an army (some said a French Navy) of helpers, and sat in the cockpit of his great 73-foot ketch, surveying the scene. He hardly spoke. He never moved. Just occasionally he barked an order, and sat watching it being carried out—the complete professional, unruffled, unhurried, totally self-contained.

When *Club Méditerranée* arrived on the Monday, an event all on its own was taking place. At 238-feet long, she is one of the largest sailing boats to be built this century. From his wheelhouse, Colas planned to survey most of the eight sails by closed circuit television. He had brought a computer which would help to tell him where he was at any time to the nearest few yards. The tricolor fluttering from the transom was about the size of *FT*'s smallest sail. The boat was alive with women—sensuous French girls with shining faces, pouting mouths and long lissome figures. I went on board one evening to see Colas, and wandered below deck to find a great cavern of a boat with no fittings of any kind—she felt like the inside of an empty cross-Channel car ferry. There was a young man in front of a stove, officially cooking a meal, at this moment in a clinch with his assistant. There were what seemed like two dozen girls sitting next to hammocks strung up between the steel bulkheads. I don't know who they were or what they were doing, but they seemed to belong on board, and as Colas came limping up to them, they all chanted in unison: 'Bonsoir Alain,' and he, like a feudal baron acknowledging the tributes of his retainers replied: 'Bonsoir mesdemoiselles.' Back in the wheelhouse, bedlam. A French couple were going at each other hammer and tongs in high-decibel French over which of them was responsible for disciplining their thoroughly undisciplined child.

On that evening, Colas was being his usual charming and friendly self. But the pressures on him finally burst out later in the week. He had dreamed of this monster machine for two years, he had organised her construction from a hospital bed after almost losing his foot in a yachting accident, he had ridden the French national (and highly nationalist) publicity machine for more than even it could take to build her and bring her to Plymouth, he had raised nearly £1m. and spent it in 12 months. For what? To win the OSTAR. And now here he was in

Plymouth, walking on a foot that had no right to be there, about to sail a boat that no one wanted to win, knowing that for him to finish second would be a terrible defeat. Quite suddenly, charming, kind, helpful Alain Colas blew a fuse. The sailing committee had quite rightly told him his computer navigation system was against the spirit of the rules and he could not use it. He held a press conference, bitterly abused the committee. This was not to be Colas's year, and perhaps he sensed it.

Michael Kane was the leading American entrant, and he too was carrying a lot on his shoulders. US Tobacco had poured money into the project. Back in America, he was being billed as the American who would win the race for America in bi-centennial year. They had made him a Stars and Stripes mainsail for the race, fitted him out with every known sort of sophisticated communications equipment. In Newport, there was a US Tobacco reception centre, the company was giving away *Spirit of America* bicentennial ballpoint pens. But there was something wrong.

Why was Kane holding press conferences calling himself the 'Muhammad Ali of the yachting world,' claiming to have logged 80,000 miles singlehanded, to have been the first person in the world to have completed a solo circumnavigation in a trimaran? There seemed to be just too much hyperbole about Michael Kane. The story of exactly what happened to Kane and his trimaran *Spirit of America* will probably never be told in full. What we know is that he returned to Plymouth after 18 days at sea claiming to have been driven back by the storms, and by various forms of damage to his boat, while 'leading the fleet.' Several months later, he told *The New York Times* that he had made tapes during the OSTAR, and when he got back to Plymouth he tried to listen to them. 'I couldn't listen any more. I broke down and cried. It all came back to me,' he was quoted as saying.

Colas and Kane were extreme cases where the pressures acting on them showed—partly at least because the demands of sponsorship thrust them into the public eye. In my case, I was very lucky—*The Financial Times* was generous, helpful and above all understanding throughout the project. The pressures that sponsorship put on me were all generated from within myself. Nevertheless, they were there. In some measure, they were there in almost all of us that week before the start. Most of us were fighting fear, nerves, pressure, tension.

The night before the race, I had a family dinner with Elizabeth, my father and stepmother and my two sisters. I was very quiet. I wanted to be on my way.

8

THE OSTAR

A minute to go to the start. A dull and almost windless day. I have spent many nightmarish hours wondering how to get away from this starting line without being hit by one of the other 81 starters in the *Jester* class or by a member of the spectator armada that has come out to watch us go. I have decided to play safe—not even to try to make a 'good' start, but to use an old trick I learned at my first Firefly week in 1958—wait at the windward end of the line until the first onrush of boats is away, then cross right up against the committee boat, tack into clear air, and use superior speed to foot past most of the rest of the fleet. I shall start under my no. 2 genoa, which I can handle easily and which does not obscure my vision. As soon as I am out in clear water, away from the spectators and the rest of the fleet, I shall put up the big genny and be on my way.

The strategy works exactly as I planned it. The gun goes, there is a great gaggle of boats all jostling for position, many of them not totally under control, much shouting. I wait with my sails flapping—there is a long way to go, and no tremendous hurry to start. After a minute, the line is beginning to clear, the spectator fleet is following the leaders. I saunter up to the line, luff up around the starting boat, several voices that I recognise shout good luck to me as I pass close underneath it, and I am away. I sail on on starboard tack for 30 yards, waiting until the area behind and to the right of me is clear of boats. Then a quick tack onto port, 50 yards in towards Cawsand, back again onto starboard, and I am just where I want to be—the windward boat in the fleet, clear of all my competitors, a light but clean south-westerly wind drifting round Penlee Point and into my sails.

FT settles down quickly, and we start climbing past most of the rest of the *Jester* fleet. I want now to head out to sea until I have enough searoom to change to my no. 1 genoa, then tack back onto port. After five minutes, a shout comes across the water—I look up and there is the cruiser with Elizabeth, my father, my stepmother and Richard McClean, *The Financial Times* advertisement director, all aboard. After half an hour, the water around me is reasonably clear of other boats. I attach the electric self-steering, hoist the inner staysail, bear away onto a close reach so that *FT* will not come about while I am changing sails, and then change swiftly from the no. 2 to the no. 1 genoa. Back to the cockpit, detach the self-steering, down staysail, tack onto port, settle her down and we're off, in almost perfect *FT* weather, with maximum sail up.

For another half hour, Elizabeth and my father motor along-side, and we chat to each other, wave a lot and make silly jokes. Then a final wave to Elizabeth—'see you in four weeks'—and I am alone. Saying goodbye to Elizabeth has been easier than I thought it would be. She at least knows what I am doing, has encouraged me to go. I find myself able without difficulty to avoid asking all the obvious questions and instead to con-centrate on the present, to look ahead to the future. 'For God's sake, go out and enjoy this race,' Elizabeth snapped at me about a month ago, when I was going through a particularly conscience-stricken few days. The message sank home deeply. I had been winding myself up into such a tight bundle of nerves, worry and guilt that I had been in danger of carrying those feelings out to sea with me.

Now, I feel that special sense of freedom that sailing always offers me, as *FT* slices through the smooth water at over 7 knots. But the feelings of release, of anticipation, the knowledge that one of my life's great adventures is just beginning, are all in-tensified by being on my own. From now on, it is me, this little boat, and whatever that great ocean out there ahead of me has to offer. Why am I doing it? I have asked myself that question so often in the last four years, and there are many answers. But in recent months, as I have found myself consciously and systematically driving out fears, brushing aside feelings that my wife and son and job are being sacrificed to my ambition to sail and win this race, I have come to see it in fairly simple terms—it is a giant ego-trip, a thoroughly selfish and self-centred venture.

Having reached an understanding of just *what* I am doing, it has not been quite so difficult in the last week or two to start behaving that way.

I look around me to see where other boats have got to. In this weather, I would expect *FT* to go fast, and behind me I see a great trail of sails representing most of my competitors. Just inshore of me is *Friends*, one of the three Dick Newick-designed Val trimarans that I know are going to provide me with serious competition. Both of us have the same waterline length of just under 28 feet. But whereas *FT* has piled weight and beam and a heavy mast and large sail area on top of this, the Vals have gone to the opposite extreme—everything is as light and as small as possible, they are under half *FT*'s weight, but carry about two-thirds her sail area. In this wind, the Val and I are going at almost identical speeds. Ahead of me is Clare Francis in *Robertson's Golly*—I am going faster than she, but she gained a few miles on me by making a much better start. I can see a couple of the Frioul 38s, entered by Marc Linski's sailing school at Marseilles. Linski came to see me aboard *FT* in Millbay dock, and told me that the five Friouls had spent the last eight months racing against each other, and that all five of them had done 8,000 miles sailing in the hands of their OSTAR skippers. They have even taller masts than *FT*, and have been built as windward machines. They are pointing far closer to the wind than *FT*, but going a little more slowly. On balance, they are marginally outsailing me, but only just. *FT* is up among the leaders of her class, and going well. That, at this stage in the race, is all I need to know.

I put her onto self-steering, and start nosing round the boat checking that everything is in order. Already, I have instinctively fallen into my singlehanded safety routine—never, under any circumstances, leave the cockpit without a safety harness on. To some singlehanders, not wearing a safety harness is a sort of virility symbol—they just never do it, and justify it to themselves by arguing that safety harnesses slow them down, get in the way. The majority follow a middle-path—they wear one in heavy weather, or when the boat is moving about, but not when everything is smooth and straightforward. To me, the risk of falling overboard is just *never* worth taking. The awful vision of

FT sailing herself away over the horizon, leaving me behind treading water, shouting and waving helplessly, has haunted me during those winter evenings when I have sat at home being far more frightened by what might happen than I ever am by what does.

FT has two jacklines running along each side of her main hull—long, continuous runs of wire to which I can attach a safety harness line as I walk up and down the boat; and I always leave the cockpit with *two* safety lines attached to my harness, a long one which I hook on for walking about the boat, and a second short one which I attach to a separate anchor point as soon as I have reached the job I have to do. In this way, the short line should stop me actually reaching the water even if I do fall over the side—I have grave doubts that I would ever get back aboard *FT* if I found myself being dragged through the water at 8 or 10 knots; while having two lines attached to two separate anchor points provides a double insurance—if one of the anchor points breaks or one of the safety lines chafes through, the second one will take over.

Now, two hours after the start, I bounce over the netting to the windward float and look over *FT*. Something is wrong. At first, it is just a sensation that reaches my brain, something that my eyes have taken in but not focused on. I look right over the boat again, but it is several seconds before I see what it is. The head of the genoa is almost into the sheave at the top of the mast. I have been winching up hard on the genoa halyard to try and take some of the fullness out of the sail forward, but I have overdone it. The Talurit splice must be actually round the block in the sheave, the snap shackle is hard up against it. The Talurit may be incurably weakened, in which case it will split, and the halyard will vanish down the mast. I hasten back to the cockpit and let go the genoa halyard enough to clear the Talurit from the sheave.

How has this happened? It is the result of a particular piece of pre-race madness that afflicted me two weeks ago. I suddenly decided that I *had* to have a new no. 1 genoa for the race. I left the order so late that Hood only succeeded in delivering it on the Thursday before the start, and we had one brief sail with it on Thursday afternoon. Now that I am using it for the first time in earnest, I am not at all happy with it. It is much fuller than its predecessor, and I am unable to get as good a shape out of it. I have been fiddling with it ever since the start, but it is still not really right. I find myself wishing I had my old one.

It takes me another day before I discover a way of hoisting and setting the sail so that it looks more or less right. In the meantime, I have checked the Talurit at the top of the genoa halyard. Though it is severely misshapen, it still appears to be sound. I am able to move the whole sail lower on the forestay to keep it away from the masthead sheave. One way and another, the problems all iron themselves out—all, that is, except for the nagging one that the sail I have taken with me is not as good as the one I have left behind.

As dusk falls on that first evening at sea, I know I am among the first four or five boats in my class; I have overcome my first serious problem; and I am approaching the area of Falmouth. In the half light, I am greeted by an immensely heartening sight —into the bay ahead of me, not pointing as high and only going marginally faster come first *ITT Oceanic*, the 128-foot schooner which finished second to Colas in the 1972 race; then *Kriter III*, formerly *British Oxygen*, the 70-foot catamaran that won the 1974 Round Britain Race. They are just half a mile ahead of me, only 100 yards apart, skippered by two Frenchmen who spend much of their lives sailing together, Yvon Fauconnier and Jean Yves Terlain. They seem almost to be sailing in convoy. Meanwhile, as dark comes down, I take one more look out to sea at *Club Méditerranée*. She has been on the horizon all afternoon. Like *ITT* and *Kriter*, she is not enjoying the light airs, and has been travelling no faster than *FT*.

Through the first night, I somehow keep awake—four times, at around midnight, my normal bedtime, my head falls onto my chest and I am woken up by the impact. As I round the Lizard, shrouded in light sea-mist, I am surrounded by other competitor's lights, although I can identify none of them. By mid-morning the following day, I am approaching the Scillies. Alain Gabbay in *Objectif Sud 3*, one of the five Frioul 38 boats, is with me. Behind, I can just make out in the haze *Friends*, the Val trimaran, another of the Frioul 38s and *Patriarche* sailed by Yves Olivaux, at 66 the oldest competitor in the race. Both *Patriarche* and *Friends* had been ahead of me before dark yesterday. I have overtaken them during the night.

Alain Gabbay and I reach the Bishop Rock Lighthouse at almost exactly the same moment. We are the first two boats in the *Jester* class, leading the other 80. As we both weather the Bishop Rock, I watch fascinated as Gabbay eases his sheets and sets a course that will take him close to Southern Ireland—he is going to take the Great Circle route. I remain close-hauled and set off just south of west for what I hope will be a fast trip to the Azores. An hour and a half later, in glorious sunshine, and feeling well satisfied with my start, I change down to the no. 2 genoa and go to sleep for four hours.

From the time I left the Scillies, I never saw another competitor until I reached Newport; and I only had one brief piece of news of a *Jester* class rival, and that was of Clare Francis when she had 1,000 miles to go. In a very real sense, I was from now on racing myself, trying to keep ahead of my target, to keep the boat going as best as I could. As I write this eight months later, I know where everyone else was, and what they were doing. On this first morning after the start, *FT* and *Objectif Sud 3* were indeed at the head of their class with Wally Green in *Friends* a short way behind us. Mike Birch in *Third Turtle* had never used his big genoa before and was a little nervous of doing so; he had made a slow start the previous day. He and Kazimierz Jaworski were both within a few miles of each other to the south of the Scillies.

Out in front, Tabarly was setting a cracking pace—in the first 24 hours, he had covered almost double the distance of *FT*. But *Club Méditerranée* was still finding the light weather difficult—she was more or less in the same position as Clare Francis after 24 hours, near the Seven Stones lightship to the north-east of the Scillies. Mike McMullen, the principal British hope for winning the race, was last seen on the evening of the start of the race, not far behind Tabarly, and at that time lying in third place. Neither he nor his boat has ever been seen or heard of since. This was to be the year when two lives were lost in the OSTAR, the first time that this has happened.

June 6-7: Second night at sea. Shortly after midnight, the wind backs from south-west to south. I am still awake to hear the 0030 shipping forecast. I set *FT* on a Great Circle course for Corvo, and find we are close reaching at 6½ knots. My strategy is working better than I had dared hope—keep her going steadily, don't exhaust yourself. But I must get some sleep tonight, I have only had four hours in the last 36. I am mildly concerned at the arrival on deck of a homing pigeon. It is clearly exhausted and hungry and lost. But I have no wish to take it with me to America. It would die before I got there. What do I do? I cannot possibly kill it, I would be haunted by visions of the wretched Ancient Mariner for the rest of the trip. But somehow, I must get rid of it. I waste a couple of hours during the night giving it water, trying to persuade it to leave *FT* while we are still close to land. It just flies back to the boat every time.

At 2 a.m., the hurricane lamp begins to flicker and die. What is the matter with that lamp? Earlier in the season it kept going out and I never did discover why. I was sent three new ones by the makers, and we finally tested two of them in Plymouth and they both ran for the whole night. Now it has gone out after just four hours. Why?

I am setting great store by the hurricane lamp. If falling overboard is the number one danger for the singlehander, then being run down by another boat is number two. It is fundamentally unseamanlike to leave a boat sailing herself with no watch. My plan is to make myself into a maritime Christmas tree at night, so that even the laziest and most sleepy watchkeeper on a merchant ship will see me. At the top of my tall mast, I have a bright, three-way navigation light lit by a single filament bulb. Also at the masthead is my Bardolph Cat's Eye radar reflector, so placed to give it maximum range and power. The hurricane lamp, however, is about fifty times as bright as the navigation lights. It is brighter even than the flashing light of a buoy. It is my safety insurance, my silent watchkeeper while I sleep.

Now it is going out. I go gingerly aft to the transom. There is no safety netting at the stern of the boat, so the procedure I adopt for moving onto the counter to play with the hurricane lamp is necessarily time consuming. I try a quick pricking

operation on the lamp—switching it off and switching it immediately back on again to clean any dirt off its plunger. I am
not quick enough, and it goes out. Back to the cabin, fiddle
around with methylated spirits, find the matches, let the
pressure out, light the meths, wait till the jet and mantle have
heated up, then pump gently, and hope the whole thing springs
to life. It is smelly work, I spill both meths and paraffin over the
chart table, the whole cabin smells like a hospital operating
theatre. After half an hour, the lamp is alight again, and I am
clambering back onto the counter to reattach it. Eventually, at
about 4 a.m., I put my head down to sleep.

The following day, it comes on to blow force five from the
South-east. I am able to keep on my course to Corvo, to leave
FT on her self-steering with the big genoa up and the main
reefed, happily planing at $8\frac{1}{2}$ knots. I feel very tired but
exhilarated. I badly need some sleep. From noon to noon since
the previous day, *FT* has sailed 185 miles on her log. The distance
on the chart is 168 miles. That is very good going.

June 8, day 4: Two bits of good news—I have got rid of the
pigeon, and have succeeded in transmitting my first message
back to London. A boat hove into view a few hours after dusk
last night, and I determined to persuade the pigeon to leave.
Five times, it took off and came back to settle on a new spot.
Five times, I shooed it away. On the fifth go, it was promptly
attacked by three seagulls, and I never saw it again—I fear it
may have flown in its panic straight into the sail, and subsequently have fallen into the sea. I do not know, and my con-
science therefore clings to the possibility that it made its way to
the passing ship.

Over the past two days, I have been periodically making
calls on Channel 16 to try and make contact with other shipping.
Today, I at last got a response. 'This is yacht foxtrot tango,
yacht foxtrot tango, does anyone receive me, does anyone
receive me?' and suddenly the little Seavoice receiver is crackling into life, and a voice comes over: 'This is *Liverpool Clipper*,
this is *Liverpool Clipper*, I receive you loud and clear.' I send a
cheerful message via the *Liverpool Clipper* to London and have a
chat with Tom Miller, the officer on the watch. The human

contact does me good, the knowledge that Elizabeth will know where I am and have less to worry about boosts my morale.

In other respects, things are not going quite so well. Yesterday evening, the wind went back to the South-west—the direction in which I want to go. I made two sail changes after dark, both of them wearing and time consuming. The sea has got shorter and more difficult, *FT* is beginning to get into her worst habits, bucking and crashing into the waves, making painfully slow progress. Instead of heading straight for Corvo, I am now being forced north of west or east of south. Neither is at all satisfactory.

I have begun to feel seasick. Not badly seasick, just slightly lethargic, knowing that if I do not stop doing whatever I am doing at the time, I may actually be sick. If that happens, then I must expect slowly to weaken over the next few days, until ultimately I am forced by continued retching and my inability to hold any food to stop and heave to for half a day while I recover. I must somehow avoid that.

Last night, I slept on and off for eleven hours. But it was interrupted sleep, and today I still feel beat. Twice during the night, I got up to relight the hurricane lamp. I have found out what is the matter—the instructions specify Aladdin Pink or some other high-quality paraffin. I bought my paraffin two days before the race at the local petrol station from a coin-in-the-slot pump. It is too dirty, the motion of the boat is stirring up the dirt, and dirt is slowly building up on the plunger until it blocks the tiny jet hole at the top. There is nothing I can do. I am going to have to keep waking up in the night, getting into oilskins, pulling on seaboots, attaching safety harness lines and fiddling about with the lamp and the meths and the paraffin. Why did I not read the instructions more carefully? It is such a stupid way to be wasting energy, and it is not even making the boat go any faster. Damn, damn, damn!

Last night, tiredness and exhaustion played strange tricks with my brain. I woke up three times convinced that Rupert Lyle was steering the boat. I lay there, listening to an orchestra playing, talking to myself about what Rupert should be doing. Rupert has done so much on the boat in the last three months, and he plays a trumpet in an orchestra. What orchestra, when, where, what am I talking about? My sleeping bag is so warm, just leave it to Rupert.

Three times I dozed off again, and the fourth time I saw the hurricane lamp flickering, and persuaded myself to emerge from the delicious warmth of the sleeping bag. Rupert—of course he is back in England. The orchestra—the Ampair wind generator is humming away in the wind, its noise rising and falling to the freshening breeze. It is so loud that it is drowning the noise of the wind in the rigging. I do not notice it during the day, because my eyes tell me in an instant how hard it is blowing. But at night, my ears take over, and the wind generator is a new noise, one that my ears do not understand at all.

My whole sleeping pattern is proving thoroughly unsatisfactory. I am trying to sleep three hours at a stretch. But I am sleeping through the alarm clock, waking up to find *FT* wallowing with too little sail up. It is taking time to get used to being at sea, for my body to adjust to what I am asking of it, time that is losing me precious miles in the race. I am supposed to be racing. Wake up. Go out onto that cold, wet deck? Come on. It's nice and warm down here. The extra sleep will do you good.

Today, I finally get up at about 8.30 a.m., much too late. The yankee and staysail are up, about twelve rolls in the mainsail, but it is only blowing force four and *FT* is moving at a miserable $4\frac{1}{2}$ knots. I get the no. 2 genoa up, shake out half the rolls, and we are soon doing over 7. Then fifteen minutes pumping the bilges. Then breakfast—Rise and Shine powdered orange juice, eggs and bacon, bread and marge and honey, a cup of coffee made from two coffee bags and powdered Coffeemate—a really thumping meal to start the day off. Then take a sunsight, work it out, transfer it onto the plotting sheet, see just how far I have gone during the night. I spend a long time poring over the chart, trying to decide where I should be going. With this south-westerly, I ought really to keep going west. But then, I shall be too close to the lows when they come across the North Atlantic, I shall be slowed down, I must keep trying to push south. I measure off the distance to Corvo, measure the angle of my optimum course. Let's try the southerly tack, and see what happens.

Into my oilskins, wet socks, pull on seaboots, up on deck.

Round onto the new tack, settle her down, adjust the Hasler vane steering. We are only making 185 degrees Magnetic, that is a true course slightly east of south. Down below again, more studies of the chart, more measuring of distances. By now I am well into the day, tuned into the BBC for background. Time to tidy up, to wash some of the more acrid parts of my body, change shirt and underpants and socks.

At about 1 p.m. the midday sunsight. This is the easy one to work out, it is not time-critical and the calculation only takes a few seconds. The midday sight gives me my latitude, and is taken when the sun is due south of me. The morning and afternoon sights give me two more 'position lines', which are roughly equivalent to a line of longitude. With three 'position lines' from my three sights, plus my knowledge of the speed and direction I have been sailing, I can work out where I am.

Today, I take my midday sight, mark it on the chart, and decide I cannot carry on with this southerly tack. I put *FT* onto the westerly tack, and wonder for the first time whether the Azores strategy really makes sense. Here I am, on a course just north of true west. It cannot possibly be right to take the southerly tack. Supposing I were to abandon the Azores, were just to carry on west, and accept the risks of stronger winds?

My answer comes almost immediately. The wind starts to rise, I change down first to cutter rig, then an hour later to the staysail and mainsail with twenty rolls in the main. By 2 p.m. it is blowing a steady force seven, *FT* is being thrown about, making no better than $4\frac{1}{2}$ knots. I decide to keep going, the wind is not strong enough to justify heaving to. I give lunch a miss, feeling that anything I eat now could trigger seasickness. The arrival of the strong wind exactly coincides with my running out of seasick tablets. Idiot! Why on earth did you not buy enough?

I am now wet and rather miserable, knowing that this is dreadful weather for *FT*, feeling how slowly she is going, imagining all those Frioul 38s slicing through it. I have been on the foredeck three times in the last three hours, the first two times to change sails, the last to tie down the yankee jib so that it does not come to any harm. The foredeck is wet and rearing about, I come back from each trip feeling a lot wetter, a little more tired, with another bout of queasiness to overcome. Reefing, too, is an exhausting and time-consuming business, rolling bits of wood into the sail, rigging up a complicated block and tackle to take bites out of the leach.

At 6 p.m., there is a great crack from on deck, I look up from my chart table and see that the staysail is collapsing. Back into oilskins, fix on safety harness lines, onto the foredeck, bring the staysail down before it flaps itself to pieces, look aloft to see what has happened. A Talurit splice on the toggle that holds the head of the sail to the halyard has broken. Luckily, the snap shackle on the end of the halyard proper has prevented the whole assembly vanishing inside the mast. But there is only one way of getting the halyard back—I have to climb the mast.

I have made elaborate plans for climbing the mast (Plate 21). I attach a climbing device called a clogger to my bosun's chair and to the tail of the spinnaker halyard. As I climb the mast, I shall slide the clogger up with me; if I fall then the clogger will immediately lock onto the spinnaker halyard, and I shall end up suspended in the bosun's chair. Built onto the mast are climbing steps, so that I can haul myself up and down without a block and tackle. As I climb, I shall hand-over-hand my two harness hooks. At any one time, therefore, I shall be held onto the mast in five separate ways—by my hands; by my feet and legs; by the clogger attached to the bosun's chair; and by the two harness lines.

It all sounded very good on land. Now, for the first time, I have to try it out, and in a force seven. The end of the staysail is 33 feet above the deck. The sea is grey and threatening with the tops breaking away from the waves. The wind is howling and whistling through the rigging. Spray is breaking into my face, water trickling down my neck. *FT* is hove to under her main, rising and falling to the seas. I stand at the foot of the mast, do one more check of all my equipment, and start to climb.

On the first attempt, I get as far as the crosstree. But because I have left the mainsail half up, I am unable to wrap my arm right round the mast. I go down again, take the main right off, find myself sweating profusely and take a couple of sweaters off as well. Then back up the mast, step by step. Slide the clogger up the halyard, lean down, unclip the lower harness line, reach up, clip it on to as high a mast step as possible, then up one more step, slide the clogger again. The higher I go, the harder it is to hold onto the mast, I am winding my arms through the mast steps, clinging to them as *FT* rolls to the sea, sending me through a wider and wider arc. A trimaran lying a-hull in a sea does not enjoy a smooth motion. She will roll with a wave, then be brought up suddenly as a float hits the water and interrupts her roll. Two multihullers—Brian Cooke and Robin Burroughs—have been wrenched away from stepped masts in the last two seasons by just this kind of sudden shock. I cling to the mast, knowing that if I let go, I shall be thrown out into space, and then smashed into the mast again by forces over which I have no control. Don't let go. Hang on. The higher I climb, the slower each movement becomes, the more I cling with arms and legs to the mast, waiting for a pause in the boat's motion before taking another step up. It is agonisingly slow, especially at the crosstree, where I have to climb round the forestay and take three steps in one movement to do so.

At last I am there, I have a hold of the halyard, I tie it onto myself, and start my way down again. The first few steps are slow as I get used to using the clogger going downwards—I have to take my weight right off it before I can release its grip and slide down the rope. But the last 20 feet I almost run down, I am on the deck, my arms are aching where they have been taking the pressure of the mast-steps. I go below, collect some bulldog clips, a wrench and a pair of pliers, go back onto the foredeck, rejoin the halyard to itself. It is still blowing force seven with the odd force eight gust. It is 10 p.m. GMT, four hours since the halyard broke, and about to get dark. I suddenly feel totally exhausted, without the energy to raise the main and the staysail and get *FT* under way again. I go below, drink a high-calory can of Nutrement, take off my wet clothes and crawl into a sleeping bag.

At midnight, I wake again. The front that produced the wind has passed through, the wind has veered to the North-west and lightened. I *must* get going. I force myself into my wet clothes and up to the foredeck, and start mechanically reeving the yankee jib onto the forestay, getting the main up, hoisting the

19 *FT*'s cockpit winch assembly: from L. to R., genoa halyard, staysail halyard/spinnaker sheet, baby winch for light runners when in use, genoa sheets, spinnaker sheet/ staysail sheets. All winches were from Gibb. Inside the cockpit is an array of quick-release cam cleats, and the fish nets which keep the tails of sheets and halyards in some sort of order.

20 *FT*'s foredeck in mid-Atlantic. The no. 2 genoa is up, the staysail is permanently hanked on to the new forestay, ready for one of its multiple uses. The big no. 1 genoa and the yankee jib are rolled up and stowed on the deck, just aft of the crossbeam.

21 My mast-climbing techni[que]
The bosun's chair is attached [to]
a self-locking Clogger (circle[d])
which slides up the spinnake[r]
halyard. The two harness lin[es]
are hand-over-handed up th[e]
mast steps, and the steps als[o]
provide holds for both my ha[nds]
and my feet. I had to climb [the]
mast three times during the
OSTAR.

22 *Third Turtle*, worthy win[ner]
of the *Jester* class in just und[er]
days. Mike Birch (above) is [a]
Canadian yacht deliverer w[ho]
lives in Devon. (*Multihull In[ter]national*)

staysail. When you are tired at sea, and especially at night, jobs that would normally take 15 or 20 minutes begin to take far longer as you pause between each movement, trying not to make a mistake, to keep yourself going. Tonight, it takes me three hours to get the sails up, to stow everything away, to get the Hasler properly adjusted, to pump out the bilges, to relight the hurricane lamp which has as usual gone out after four hours. It is 3 a.m. on June 9 before I go back to sleep, leaving *FT* sailing a course of 220 degrees at $6\frac{1}{2}$ knots. That, I tell myself, cannot be bad. Besides, I feel the threat of seasickness receding. If I was going to be seasick, today would have been the day, and I have survived it.

June 10, day 6: In mid-morning, disaster strikes. My log stops working. At first, I feel no concern. It has often stopped before and is easy to repair. First, I clean the underwater assembly—it has probably got weed or dirt on it. No good. Then I replace the whole underwater unit. Still no good. Whatever has gone wrong it is a new fault.

I have never sailed alone without a log, and I have come to rely on it, not only for navigating but more important for telling me how fast I am going. At night in particular, I find speed through the water very hard to gauge, and I need the speed-ometer to help me keep her going near her optimum.

I spend the whole afternoon trying to take an intelligent interest in the instrument's electrical circuit. It is a little like trying to converse with an Arab out of a guidebook—I have just the barest inkling of what I am doing, but no understanding whatever. I check every connection, unscrew lots of wires, and screw them back into place again. Nothing seems to be out of place. Nothing that I do makes any difference. By 4 p.m., I am deep into a bout of self-pity, cursing the instruments, raging at the weather. The wind just goes on and on blowing from the South-west, the sea is tossing *FT* around, the light airs that I need to win this race have vanished. Now, I have no log, no speedometer, at night I shall have to slow *FT* right down, the race is as good as over.

For half an hour, I allow myself to dissolve into self-pity and paranoia. Then, I manage to take a grip of myself. I decide to have one last go at finding what is wrong before dark. As I calm myself down, I find my eyes resting on a little black box beneath the instruments. The box is new, it was installed at the beginning of the season as an 'improvement'. It is sealed, with five coloured wires connected into it. What, I ask myself, is inside?

I open up my knife, sharpen it, start cutting into the sides of the two by three-inch plastic box. The sea is buffeting the boat about, my hand is unsteady, I worry that whatever is inside, I may harm it. After half an hour of patient cutting, I take the front off, and find behind it a tiny printed circuit board. Somebody once told me that if a printed circuit board goes wrong, you should scrape the contacts and spray the whole thing with a can of Servisol. On that slender evidence, I went out and bought a can of Servisol, and have been carrying it on board ever since. I aim the can at the circuit board, and fire. Immediately, the speedometer springs to life and registers a speed of 7 knots. A minute later, it goes dead again. But at last I know what the trouble is. Somewhere in that printed circuit board is a loose or corroded connection.

Never has a circuit board been treated with such love and respect. Every single metal contact is scraped. Sure enough, two of them have been corroded by sea water. A quarter of a can of Servisol is sprayed over the six square inches of micro-circuitry. Then, the whole assembly is closeted behind an array of plastic bags, to prevent any water, or even a hint of dampness, from ever reaching it again. At 8.30 that evening, $9\frac{1}{2}$ hours after the log had gone on the blink, I write: 'Log really working.' Dinner that night is a really cracking one: Cornish prawn soup, rognons sautés, Surprise peas, a dollop of Smash, banana and chocolate, all washed down with a can of beer (the only alcohol I have on board). I am over the seasickness, over a bad crisis, thoroughly pleased with myself.

June 12, day 8: At midday today, I have been at sea exactly a week, and am about 800 miles from the start. Corvo is 500 miles to the South-west of me. I feel I must get there in 12 days if I am to have a chance of meeting my 28-day target. I am charting my progress daily against that of *Cap 33*, *Three Cheers* and *Toucan* in 1972, using their races as a benchmark. *Cap 33* and *Three*

Cheers were past Corvo in 11 days, *Toucan* in 12. Twelve, therefore, is my absolute maximum.

Any doubts I had about my 'southern strategy' have been dispelled by this first week. After a very good first three days, *FT* was stopped dead by that force seven on Tuesday, and has not been going well ever since. There is a short Atlantic chop around, not the swell that I had been led to expect. But the wind never leaves the South-west—for three days now, I have been continuously close hauled on port tack, heading roughly west, but not making anything like the progress I would like. On Wednesday, 120 miles; on Thursday, 120; in the last 24 hours, 117. I am averaging rather more than this on the log— just over 6 knots, or about 148 miles through the water. But the seas are knocking *FT* about a lot, and the self-steering, which cannot anticipate seas, is overcompensating. We are slaloming through the water, losing distance and time. The wind is generally force five or six, just too much for *FT* to enjoy, but luckily not so much as to stop her. I long for lighter weather and calmer seas. Hurry on, the Azores!

Today has been a big clean-out day. I checked my fresh water and there seemed to be plenty, so I have had my first all-over wash—standing in the cabin allowing the water and the soap to just run off me into the bilges. At the end of it all, I washed my hair for good measure—a big morale booster. But I did not shave. I never shave at sea, it is the one chance I get to grow a rather unimpressive and scraggly beard. Then I went for a complete change of clothes—clean and dry everything, even to dry trousers. It is nearly a week since I knew what dry trousers felt like. Then, I embarked on a major clean-out: overboard went Reed's Nautical Almanac (finished with it), two cushions (sodden and unlikely ever to dry—I find my spare sleeping bag a far more comfortable pillow), four books (sodden, and I'm not finding time to read anyway), and the washing up liquid (I wash up in sea water). After that I attacked the food— out went eight cans of beer, a pot of Bovril, and various packets of biscuits. I still have over ten gallons of water, but for the time being I shall hang on to that just in case.

My mood varies very much with the day. Yesterday, my hands were so sore from cuts that would not heal that I put a plastic bag over the left hand to try and protect it. The wind was all over the place, and there was not much of it; *FT* just slopped around, and I kept going up on deck to change sails. Nothing changed after dark. I spent all night up on deck, as the wind gradually increased from force two to force five. At 6 a.m., I finally got to bed.

FT then sailed herself like a real pro for six hours. I kept waking up and checking her, and each time I looked, things were getting better, the wind was backing all the time, and freeing me. When I finally took a sight at midday, we were further south than I had dared hope, and still plugging through the sea westwards at about 7 knots. This afternoon as I write this, I am full of hope. Corvo is only 500 miles away—I *must* be able to do that in five days, and then I shall be past it in twelve, I shall be south of the Gulf Stream, in light airs and smoother seas. Then just watch *FT* go! Yesterday, I knew I had had it, I knew the race was lost. Today, I am dreaming of winning again. Even the cuts on my hands are showing signs of forming their own calluses at last.

June 14, day 10: The storm that cut through the fleet on June 14 was the worst ever experienced in this race. By the time it had blown itself out, it had ineradicably altered the whole nature of the 1976 OSTAR. The results of all three classes were more or less decided by what happened on and in the two days after June 14.

The cause of all the trouble was a particularly deep low that swept into the North Atlantic from Newfoundland in the early hours of June 13, went very close to the leading boats, and then peeled off North to Greenland. When the low hit the fleet—the fourth in less than a week—*Club Méditerranée* had a commanding lead. By the time it had gone, her sails were blown out and she had slowed right down. *Gauloises*, a long, slim 52-footer near the front of the *Gipsy Moth* fleet, sank, and her skipper Pierre Fehlmann, was involved in a dramatic rescue at the height of the storm. One of *ITT Oceanic*'s winch handles flew out of control and so badly injured Yvon Fauconnier that he had to give up, and abandon the massive 128-foot schooner in mid-ocean. (She was subsequently recovered and sailed to St Johns,

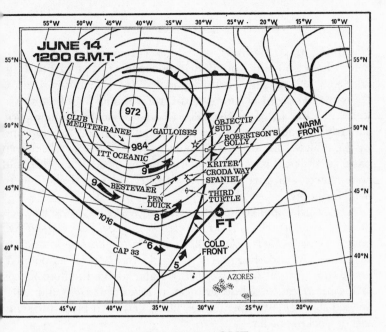

10 June 14, 1200 GMT.

The gale that decimated the fleet. You see here a classic North Atlantic storm, with a deep low at its centre, and sharp increases in the barometric pressure over relatively short distances causing high winds. The wind strengths were actual reports from ships in the area. A depression of this severity is rare in the month of June.

At 1200 hours, the low was moving rapidly north-north-east. An hour later, the cold front passed over *FT*, causing a 30 degree wind shift, and by the following day, *FT* was enjoying north-westerlies (in the northern hemisphere, the wind blows anti-clockwise round the centre of a depression, more or less parallel to the direction of the isobars). *Cap 33* was already among the north-westerlies, and was well away from the centre of the low. All the other leaders were in very strong winds indeed. Alain Colas on *Club Méditerranée*, the boat nearest the centre of the low, reported winds of force 10 (48–55 knots), and tore many of his sails. *Gauloises* first sprang a leak, and was then knocked down, breaking her mast. *ITT Oceanic* had retired six hours earlier, but was riding out the storm with a badly injured and immobile skipper. *Kriter* was beginning to fall apart. Both *Bestevaer* and *Croda Way* sustained damage that forced them to turn back to Plymouth. *Third Turtle*, *Spaniel*, *Objectif Sud* and *Robertson's Golly* all had to heave to for up to two days. *Pen Duick* was blown back on her tracks. Mike McMullen's father, Captain Colin McMullen, believes that it may have been this storm that turned *Three Cheers* over. Mike had talked often about taking a far northern route, heading for the Belle Isle Strait and passing round the back of Newfoundland. If he was on this course, and going well, this low may have passed right over him. If he was nearer the traditional Great Circle route, then he could have been somewhere in the triangle formed by *Club Méditerranée*, *ITT Oceanic* and *Gauloises*. I must emphasise that this is pure speculation, since there were no sightings of *Three Cheers* after the first day of the race.

Newfoundland). *Kriter III*, the 70-foot catamaran that two years before had won the Round Britain Race, started to break up and was left to sink. *Bestevaer*, sailed by Dutchman Gerard Dijkstra, damaged her mast and turned round for Plymouth—she was lying third in the fleet when the storm hit her. Eric Tabarly, already demoralised by the loss of his self-steering and by the effort of handling his huge spreads of canvas, was driven back 50 miles. The metal crossbeams on *Croda Way*, *FT*'s old rival, started to part company with her float, and she had to head for home.

All my principal competitors in the *Jester* class were stopped dead in their tracks—*Third Turtle*, *Spaniel*, *Friends*, *Objectif Sua* and *Robertson's Golly*. Mike Birch in *Third Turtle* spent nearly two days hove to. Kazimierz Jaworski in *Spaniel* was pooped, and found himself with two feet of water above the floorboards of his main cabin. Clare Francis in *Robertson's Golly* damaged her self-steering, and spent many hours getting it back into some sort of working order.

FT missed the storm entirely. Of the eventual prizewinners, only *FT* and *Cap 33* did so. I was 600 miles from the centre of the storm, and 250 miles south of most of my competitors. On the night of June 13–14, I had a foggy, wet, unpleasant night—nothing worse. I had no knowledge of what was happening to the north of me. I was out of range of the BBC and did not have the right equipment to pick up the special shipping forecasts that had been laid on for the race. I heard nothing about the storm of June 14 until I arrived in Newport.

This is how my log records the low as it passed to the north of me: 'June 13–14: Fairly typically unpleasant sort of night. At 2300 GMT, visibility is down to about 50 yards, the wind blowing 25 knots across the deck. I am down to yankee jib and staysail, and about 12 rolls. Turn the foghorn on and leave it on for the night.

'2330: Wind alarm goes set at 30 knots. I reset it and go back to bed.

'Midnight: Wind alarm goes again. Take in more rolls on main. Redo hurricane lamp.

'0300: Wind alarm goes set at 32 knots. Reset it, but it goes again before I am back in my sleeping bag. Get up and into wet

clothes and oilskins. Take in more rolls on main. I have trouble
getting *FT* to balance, but finally get her moving.

'0530: More wind alarm calls, with alarm set on 34 knots.
Wind now beginning to blow force seven. Hand yankee jib and
leave her under main and staysail. She is undercanvassed but
comfortable, wallowing a bit at 4½ knots.

'0830: Wind is now a steady 32 knots, boat going quite well at
5½–6 knots due west.

'0930: Get up for the day. Pump out boat. Adjust sails. Have
breakfast. A thoroughly wet, unpleasant and disturbed night.'

After breakfast, I put the yankee back up, and keep *FT* going
hard into the sea all morning. At 1300, the following entry
appears in my log:

'1300: Front passes through. Wind veers 30 degrees. Tack onto
southerly tack, course 200. Wind very light for a while, but then
comes in at about 16 knots from North-west. No. 2 genoa and
full main all afternoon.'

And that, so far as *FT* was concerned, was the end of the
June 14 storm.

Somewhere out in the middle of the ocean, two men lost their
lives. *Galloping Gael*, a 38-foot monohull sailed by Mike
Flanagan, was found with her mainsail half up and nobody
aboard. Mike Flanagan, married with several children, was
lost overboard, probably washed or knocked over while reefing
his mainsail. Mike McMullen's loss was part of a double
tragedy. His wife Lizzie was electrocuted in an accident while
working on *Three Cheers* three days before the start. The 1976
race claimed a total of four lives—Lizzie McMullen and Brian
Cooke also died in pursuit of victory in the OSTAR. The race
would not be what it is without danger. It will claim more
lives in the future. Every time it does so, it will leave sadness and
a sense of loss behind.

At 1300 hours on June 14, the wind veered through 30 degrees.
It was precisely the moment when the cold front stretching
southwards from the storm centre passed over me. It was also,
I believe, the moment when I lost any chance of winning the
Jester trophy. I had held the firm conviction that my route was to

the Azores and south of the Gulf Stream. The Gulf Stream flows due east at up to 3 knots in places. I had seen it as a silent and invisible barrier between the northern and southern fleets, leaving us in our separate weather systems, before we came together again just before Newport.

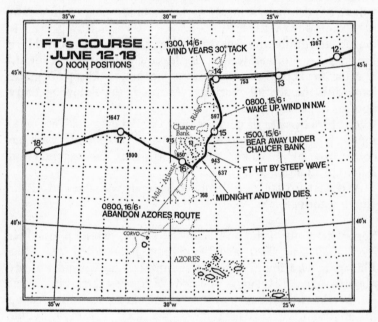

11 *FT*'s course, June 12–18.

At 1300 hours on June 14, I had been close-hauled on port tack for five days—the wind had blown relentlessly from the south-west, usually between force five and force six. In these winds and these seas, *FT* is no more than an adequate performer—I had just kept plugging on, knowing that I was not putting up a good time, waiting for the conditions to change so that *FT* could show herself at her best. If only, I kept saying to myself, I could get south, down to the lighter winds, the calmer seas. My whole thinking was south, south, south.

When the wind went through 30 degrees as the front passed over me, I did not think twice about what to do. I tacked

immediately. My course on the southerly tack was not a particularly good one—about 185 degrees true, just west of south.
But Corvo was 380 miles away, with a bit of luck I could get
there in three days, and stay within my 12-days-to-Corvo
target. Even if I got there in 13 days, then I would only have
a day to make up, I could do that with a bit more luck than I
had had with the first 10 days' weather.

It was a mistake. Two days later, I had abandoned my
southern strategy, and had adopted instead a different plan that
had been forced on me—the 'Gulf Stream strategy'. In the
three days from midday on June 14 to midday on June 17, my
real progress towards Newport was only 230 miles. By sticking
with my Azores strategy too long, I had 'lost' at least 100 miles.

Now, of course, it is all so clear. But at the time, I did not
know that *Third Turtle* and *Spaniel* were hove to 250 miles to
the north of me, riding out their storm. I did not know that
once I was over the Mid-Atlantic Ridge—and I was almost on
it at the time—the seas would become longer and flatter, and
FT would thoroughly enjoy her sail through the Gulf Stream;
I did not know that 38 hours later, the winds would go back to
the south-west, and force me to abandon the Azores idea altogether. Above all, I had never examined the arithmetic of the
Gulf Stream route—how much current I should expect, how
much distance I would save by taking it. When four days later
I did so, I came up with some startling results. Therein lies the
fascination of this race. You take decisions days or months in
advance, but you cannot possibly tell when you take them what
their long-term effects will be. At some point, Birch and
Jaworski and Greene and Gabbay and Clare Francis had taken
decisions that had led them into the June 14 storm. Now,
unknown to me, I had a chance to go back into the lead among
the *Jester* boats. I did not take it. For the next ten days, *FT*
snapped at the heels of the two leaders *Third Turtle* and *Spaniel*
to the north of her. But she never again led them.

June 15, day 11: I wake up to find I have slept through the
alarm clocks. The wind has changed, *FT* has put herself about,
and is stationary. Even when I realise this, it takes me half an
hour to persuade myself to get up. Awful. When I get up, it is

to find a north-westerly wind has come in, and is blowing quite hard. How long have I been like this? How long have I been wasting this lovely north-westerly? I am furious with myself, enraged at my laziness and incompetence. Why did I let myself get so tired yesterday? I kept changing sails, as the wind died, then came up again, then died. It all got me nowhere, and now a real wind has come in, from the direction that I want it, and I have slept through it.

I take a sunsight, and a moonsight. They are not very easy ones, there is a heavy swell running. But with two position lines, I can get a fairly precise plot. The sights show me to be fifty miles further east than I thought I was (hoped I was?). Am I feeling the Gulf Stream? Have I been making leeway? Is my compass accurate? For whatever reason, there are fifty more miles to America than I thought.

All morning, *FT* makes good progress, heading on a true course of almost due south-west. At 2 p.m. I try to get a noon-sight. I am sailing through the largest swell I have ever seen, the waves rolling at me like moving mountains, long, slow rollers that make finding the horizon for a sunsight an act of faith. I spend an hour at the chart; it looks as if I am sailing straight at the Chaucer Bank. Now what do I do?

The Chaucer Bank is marked on my chart as having a minimum depth of 13 fathoms. It is the shallowest part of the Mid-Atlantic Ridge, an almost sheer underwater mountain. On either side of it, the water is about a mile deep. But the bottom shelves almost vertically, and at its peak, the underwater mountain is just 80 feet below the surface. I dare not sail straight over it. These enormous seas could be breaking on it. I have two choices—I can either tack back onto port, in which case I shall probably find myself pointing almost due north; or I can bear away onto a reach, pass under the lee of the Chaucer Bank, and then harden up as soon as I am clear. That way, I shall keep on heading south, and at the rate I am going today, I am going to be past Corvo in my 12-day target time anyway.

I bear away onto a 65 degree reach, so that the waves are at almost 90 degrees to *FT*'s course. *FT* glides up the backs of the waves, heeling over to them, climbing them slowly as they roll towards her, the occasional wave breaking at the crest. As the crest of the wave passes under her, it first gently lifts the weather float, then quickly comes through to the centre hull and goes on to the lee float, and now we are heeling over towards the wind as we slide down the wave's face. The speedometer shows a steady 8½ knots, the wind about 25 knots.

I am below, working at the chart table. The waves are getting steeper, give the appearance of being taller. I have had to take the main sheet out of the sheet release system, because we are heeling at such a sharp angle as we climb up the waves that the sheet kept flying unnecessarily. We are now under the lee of the Chaucer Bank, these waves must be building up over it.

Suddenly, I am thrown backwards, everything on the chart table is on the cabin floor, I am trying to recover my balance, reaching for the main sheet to release it. A wave had come through and broken under the weather float, and the breaking top has rolled on into the main hull, and pushed us further over. To this day, I do not know how far *FT* went over, how near she came to capsizing, just that it was all terribly sudden, that by the time I had collected myself together enough to do anything about it, the danger was past, the lee float had come back up again, and we were sliding down the face of the wave into the deep trough between it and the next one.

By 1900 hours, we are past the Chaucer Bank, I am hardening up again, still dreaming of Corvo, now 200 miles to the Southwest of me. By midnight, the wind has died—just gone, vanished. There is nothing to do but down sails, whistle at the beautiful, star-filled night, and go to sleep.

June 16, day 12: The steep seas of yesterday are today a long, languid swell. There is just the trace of a wind—from the Southwest. I try starboard tack—the compass reads 175 degrees. I try port tack—the compass reads 310. That is a tack through 135 degrees. I go back onto starboard, and try steering her myself. I can do no better than the electric self-steering. What is the matter with *FT*? She must point higher than this. I start cursing the new genoa, it must be the sail's fault, why did I not take the old one? A course of 175 Magnetic is a true course of 160. That is 20 degrees east of south, I cannot, I must not go on this tack. Corvo, instead of being just a day's sail away is suddenly two, three, even four days away.

I go into rapid mental decline. There is no way now that I can win this race, my whole southern strategy has failed. I cannot go on going south in this wind. I must tack and go west. Wait, wait half an hour, think it through, in this wind there is no urgency for a decision, just calm down and try and think rationally about what you are doing. I look at a picture of Elizabeth and James, and start berating myself for coming on this race. What is the point of being here, of taking all these risks, when now I am going to arrive in Newport way down the fleet, the boat that started favourite and ended nowhere. What will I say to *The Financial Times*? How will I face my colleagues when I get back? 'I tried to go South but I couldn't, the wind just kept blowing from the South-west.' They will only understand, that the paper put money up for this man who said he could sail a boat, and it turned out he could not.

I keep trying to take a grip on myself, trying to stop paranoia overwhelming me. Outside, the sun is already beating down from a blue sky, it is going to be a blistering day. But where is the wind? Why from the South-west? What is the matter with *FT*, she has always pointed so close to the wind before, now she is over 65 degrees off it?

I take out my three pictures of the family, and stare at them for several minutes. Elizabeth is going to be in Newport, I must get to Newport, I must head west. If I go on south, it will be 14, 15 days before I am past Corvo. That would mean Newport in 30 days at the earliest. It is just out of the question. Head west. Make the best you can of the boat and sails you have got. Sail through the Gulf Stream.

I grab the ocean currents chart. It shows quite clearly that the Gulf Stream runs much weaker to the North than to the South. If I aim to sail between 41 and 42 degrees north latitude, then I should have an average of less than a knot a day against me. That is 18–20 miles a day, perhaps 8 miles a day more than for boats north of the Gulf Stream, who still have to contend with about half a knot of North Atlantic drift. That's not too bad. Let's start heading west and see what happens.

The decision takes nearly an hour. At last I take it. Unless there is some radical wind change during the day, I shall abandon my southern strategy. From now on, I shall take a route that nobody has ever consciously taken before—straight through the Gulf Stream. I shall aim to stay between 41 degrees and 42 degrees latitude. I must not go further north—up north, there is wind, cold, fog and icebergs. I dare not go south—that would be to invite the Gulf Stream to do its worst. I tack and head west.

Only now do I notice that the VHF aerial at the top of the mast has come loose. It is swinging wildly round and round, threatening to hit the Baron wind vane at the top of the mast. If it does so, the wind vane will be broken, I shall have no wind alarm left to wake me up when the wind rises in the night.

I decide to climb the mast while we are moving—enough time has already been wasted today. But I cannot make it to the top. Even in this dead light wind, the shock of the boat rising and falling to the swell is threatening to throw me off the mast. I find myself clutching the mast with all my strength about ten feet from the top, yelling my son's name, urging myself to go down, take the sails down and start again. The whole process takes another hour, an hour when we are stationary. By that time, there is an 8-knot breeze, and *FT* sets off towards America at over 7 knots. She has found her light weather.

June 16 was the low point. There are usually low points in singlehanded sails, when it all suddenly gets on top of you, and you cannot get out from underneath. Mine always seem to be associated with too little wind rather than too much. There were other low points during the trip—that first day of heavy winds when I had to climb the mast was one, the day the log broke was another. But having gone through a real trauma on the morning of the 16th, I pulled myself together very quickly. I had various mechanisms for doing this. One was to think of the finish, of meeting Elizabeth, of the holiday we planned together. Another was to fantasize about the future, about my son growing up, teaching him to sail, watching him win a race for the first time, about all the time I would have to spend with him when the *FT* project was over.

Then, in the strange dual personality that I seem to split into as soon as I am alone at sea, there was the bit of me that was truly appalled at the spectacle of me breaking down under pressure. Even at the low points, there was lurking just beneath the depression a person who was determined to reach Newport, to win the race, to throw off the despondency. 'Take a grip on yourself,' I said to myself out loud on the morning of the 16th. 'Get the charts out, measure your options, and in half an hour take a decision.' That bit of me had a hard fight on its hands on the 16th. But in the end, it won.

The recovery time from depression at sea, like from seasickness, is almost immediate. After my trip up the mast, *FT* settled down to one of the most perfect day's sailing I ever had with her. The sun shone. The wind slowly increased during the day to 15 knots. As it did so, *FT* started pointing close to the wind again. Her performance earlier in the day had been a response to the combination of light airs and the heavy swell and nothing to do with the much abused genoa.

By mid-afternoon, I had changed down to the no. 2 genoa. The long, slow swell of the morning gradually flattened out as I left the Mid-Atlantic Ridge behind me. The sea was a deep Gulf Stream blue, glistening under the sun. My average speed during the day was 7 knots.

By the evening, I was writing lyrical notes in my log, listing every job I had done during the day: 'transferred five gallons from jerry can into tank; tightened backstay; oiled hanks on nos. 1 and 3 genoas; mended one of Tillermaster self-steering gears; checked both floats for water in all three compartments—they were almost dry'. I was describing the day's sail, cooking a dinner of fricandeau de riz. But more important I had made a detailed study of the 'Gulf Stream route' to see what it all added up to. I had discovered that by heading west, I was 'saving' over 200 miles of distance. I expected to be in the Gulf Stream for about 12 days, whereas on the Azores route, I would be in it for about three days. I would need, therefore, to have an average contrary current of $1\frac{1}{2}$ knots for the 'Gulf Stream route' to work out worse than the 'Azores route'. In terms of wind, I should expect more wind on the route I had now been forced into than on the Azores route—but the risk of running out of it altogether was less.

Just before the start, I had been sent a most interesting

article about the Gulf Stream. I had always imagined it as a 300-mile stretch of warm blue water flowing at a uniform speed in a uniform direction. The article told me that this was quite wrong. The Gulf Stream is indeed warm and blue. But the main current—the bit that flows at up to 3 knots—is only a few miles wide, and snakes through the water like a river. The trick of Gulf Stream sailing is to avoid getting caught by this fast moving water, which can be travelling north or south or even occasionally west as it curls its way across the Atlantic. If I stayed north of 41 degrees I felt I had a reasonable chance of missing the Stream's main force.

With the benefit of hindsight, I can see just how right the decision to go west was. I *did* manage to avoid the worst of the Gulf Stream current until the last three days, when I may have 'lost' as much as 80 miles. On the morning I took the 'Gulf Stream' decision (June 16), three boats were at about the same longitude as me and heading for the southern route. They were *Venilia*, a 54-foot Italian monohull; *Tahiti Bill*, Bill Howell's 43-foot catamaran on her third OSTAR; and *Azulao*, a light-weight *Jester* class trimaran. All three of them headed on south, and all of them lost heavily to *FT*. *Venilia* was to finish two days after me, *Tahiti Bill* five days, and *Azulao* eight days. All of them complained of too light winds.

But that is the fascination of this race. It contains so much, it tests at so many levels—seamanship, the ability to make a boat go fast, stamina, character, organisation, pre-planning. Then, at the end of all that, it throws in a great dollop of luck. There is no 'right way' to go if you want to win. But the winner always goes 'the right way'.

For the four days from June 17 to June 21, I averaged 130 miles a day on the chart. My distance through the water was even more spectacular—an average of 172 miles a day. They were days when everything seemed to go right. My log is full of the little notes that the singlehander scribbles down when he and the boat are at one with each other and he is enjoying himself. 'June 17: Wind has backed further to south-south-west. We are *creaming* along due west or slightly south of it at between $7\frac{1}{2}$ and 8 knots. I have eased the sheets—just 2 inches, but it is ten days since I last eased my sheets, ten days of solid windward bash. June 18: Half way dinner; asparagus tips plus mayonnaise; poulet chasseur plus spinach plus Smash plus mushrooms à la crème; Heineken (to reach the poor neglected parts that other beers . . .); orange; chocolate. June 20: The best night we've had. We have done 90 miles in less than 12 hours, average 7½ knots' and then, as a north-easterly came in and I started surging at up to 12 knots: 'Wind and current chart says there is a half per cent chance of my having this lovely wind.'

The mood could alter quite quickly. 'June 19: Very bad night; squalls followed by calms, the worst possible prescription for singlehandling.' Or: 'Had to change sails just after dark. Took 1¾ hours from beginning to end of changing down from main and no. 2 to double reefed main and two headsails. Just a long, thoroughly wet job. I am beginning to be bored, and to want very much to arrive. That foredeck is just a thoroughly unpleasant place.'

That was the beginning of two days of strong westerlies, days when I was slowed right down, and only managed 180 miles in 48 hours. 'June 22: I feel the race slipping away from me. I thought I would avoid these strong winds in this latitude.' But on June 23, the weather improved, we were on our way again. 'I'm on a *reach* again. Sheets eased. On course for Newport. Speed 7 knots. I can win after all.'

I was enjoying the sail. Not all of it, but most of it. I was now on the finish chart, which covered the area from 43 degrees west to Newport. I marked a series of little vertical lines for every 200 miles from Newport—1200 miles to go, 1,000, 800, 600.

I was finding on this, only my second real singlehanded sail, how much I love the sea and being on it. Those days when things were going well, when the sea was a lovely shade of deep blue, when the sun was out, the sails drawing, when the loudest noises were the gentle whisper of the boat as she rose and fell to the waves, the gurgle of the water as it flowed past the hull— those were days when I felt a degree of peace with myself and my surroundings that I have never known on land. I was never bored—there was always too much to do, sails to change, clothes to wash, sights to take, meals to cook, charts to work on, things to repair. Because of this, I was never lonely, in the sense of suddenly longing for company. This is all the more curious for the fact that on land, I find my own company unbearably dull. But at sea, there is a chemistry operating between myself and a sailing boat and the water that I only dimly understand; and when I am alone, all these feelings are intensified, the feeling of completeness, of being in control of one's destiny, of carelessness.

Paradoxically, I listened to the radio a lot. It was a sort of background noise, like music at a dinner party. There was an economic summit in Kingston, riots in Soweto, droughts in England, we seemed to be in a continuous state of losing a test match. Normally, I live with this news, feed off it like a drug. Back in London, I am woken by a clock radio with the 7.30 news, I sit for two hours before going to work reading eight newspapers, I spend all day producing tomorrow's *Financial Times*. But out in the ocean, surrounded by sun and wind and sea and sky, my only visitors the occasional school of porpoises playing and squeaking around my three hulls, I listened to what was going on in the world that I had left behind and felt no part of it. I tried once to imagine myself at Bracken House, surrounded by telephones, reams of agency tape crossing my desk, taking a series of instant decisions that would shape the next day's paper. I could not do it. That person had been left behind on shore.

It had taken some time for me to get used to being at sea. During the first week when seasickness was haunting me, when my hands were sore, when I constantly slept through alarm clocks, when I had strange illusions of someone else on board with me, my body was not yet adjusted to it. But after three weeks away, I was in most respects completely attuned to my surroundings. If the weather was changeable, and I wanted to wake up in 90 minutes, I would sleep for precisely 89. But if I was tired, and the weather seemed settled, I would not put the alarm clock on at all. Quite often, I would wake out of these deep sleeps and wonder where I was.

I was able to luxuriate in these very deep sleeps for two quite distinct reasons. First, I could not take seriously the possibility of being run down in mid-ocean. I would wake up, remember where I was, see that the sky was still blue, and lie in my sleeping bag warning myself that there just might be a ship about to run me down. Myself was quite unmoved. 'But it could be a 250,000-ton tanker,' I told myself (almost all my dialogue with myself when alone at sea is out loud). Myself could not imagine such a thing. The ocean is so vast, and *FT* so small, and this tiny little world in which the two of us were living was so private that I simply could not persuade myself that a collision in broad daylight and in mid-ocean was possible.

The second reason was that by the end of the first ten days, I had come to love and to rely on two pieces of equipment that I had had no trust in at all at the start—the wind-speed alarm and the sheet-release system. The wind-speed alarm I could set at any wind speed. If the wind reached that speed for only a split second while I was asleep, the alarm would start to whine, and would not stop until I had got up and turned it off. My rule was that the first time it went, I got up, reset it and went back to the sleeping bag again. The second time, I had to get up, put on my wet clothes and oilskins, pull on my boots, go up on deck and change sails. I was woken far more often by the wind speed alarm than I was by the alarm clock.

Before the start, I had so little faith in the sheet-release system that I almost left it behind. But after a certain amount of adjusting in the first week, it too performed well. Its only fault was that it was over-eager—it let my sheets go too often. On about ten separate occasions, I woke up to find the mainsail flapping and *FT* wallowing. But that, in a multihull, is a fault on the right side.

As I gradually built up faith in these two pieces of equipment, so I was able to go to sleep leaving *FT* going much faster, especially in light weather. On the second afternoon of the race, as I sailed away from the Scilly Isles, I had changed down from no. 1 to no. 2 genoa to go to sleep. Now, after three weeks at sea, I was quite regularly going to sleep under full sail.

All these factors made *FT*'s performance over the second half of the course far more impressive than over the first. She did the first half in 14 days, the second in 13. Of more importance, between June 17 and June 22, *FT* was gradually catching up the two *Jester* boats ahead of her—*Third Turtle* and *Spaniel*.

In the first ten days, when I had been getting so depressed about *FT*'s performance, *FT had* gone slowly. When the June 14 storm hit the leaders, *FT* was two to three days behind them. From the moment that *FT* adopted her 'Gulf Stream strategy', she was always in the hunt. By June 22, she was about half a day behind *Third Turtle* and *Spaniel*. I knew nothing of these two boats. All I knew was that on June 23, Clare Francis had reported herself to be 1,000 miles from the finish—exactly the same distance to go as *FT*. I had assumed then—and had spent a rather miserable afternoon thinking about it—that if Clare and I were on level terms, then there must be some other boats ahead of me, probably one of the Frioul 38s. *Robertson's Golly* was by no means the fastest boat in the *Jester* class, and I had never before now considered her a serious rival. I had also over-estimated the challenge of the Frioul 38s. Only two of the five were to finish, and the leading one, *Objectif Sud III*, was never more than a day ahead of me. She was to finish fifth, over a day behind *FT*. Among the bigger boats, Tabarly in *Pen Duick* was sailing doggedly on towards Newport. Nobody was more sur-prised than Tabarly when he eventually learned he had won in the very slow time of 23 days 20 hours. But his rivals were all dropping out. Alain Colas in *Club Méditerranée* had put into St Johns to repair sails. Tom Grossman in *Cap 33* broke a tension strut on one of his three beams, and then got himself into a navigational tangle and spent two days going backwards—I suspect that tiredness and inexperience cost him what would have been a thrilling and exciting victory. In the *Gipsy Moth* class, with no *Gauloises*, no *Bestevaer* and no *Three Cheers*, Jean Claude Parisis in *Petrouchka* was now leading.

My tactics during the last third of the race were governed by three factors: first, I wanted to stay far enough south to avoid the centres of the lows that tend to sweep across Nova Scotia and Newfoundland and out into the Atlantic; secondly, I wanted to stay away from the fog and icebergs on the Grand Banks; thirdly, and much the most important factor, the pre-vailing winds for the last, 1000 miles are south-westerly. I wanted to stay as close as possible to the latitude of Newport, so that when the south-westerlies came, I would not have to beat straight into them. I knew that in doing this, I faced stronger currents in the Gulf Stream; and that I was missing the chance to take advantage of the favourable Labrador Current which flows from the Grand Banks down towards Newport and New York.

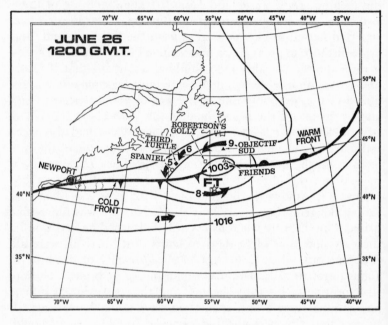

12 June 26, 1200 GMT.

The gale that decided the result of the *Jester* Trophy. A shallow and developing low was moving along the edge of the warm Gulf Stream current where it met the cold Labrador current. The wind speeds shown were actual reports from ships at 1200 GMT. Fifteen minutes later, *FT* was hit by a squall which gave a reading of 50 knots on her anemometer. The low passed the two *Jester*-class leaders, *Spaniel* and *Third Turtle*, before it was fully developed. By 1200, the worst was already well behind them, and they were both enjoying medium–strong following winds. Over the next 24 hours, *Third Turtle* was to take the lead from *Spaniel*, and keep it to the finish. *Robertson's Golly* and *Friends* were both near the centre of the low. But while *Friends* rode it out quite comfortably, Clare Francis seriously damaged her self-steering, and had to slow right down for the final week of the race. David Houghton, head of the London Weather Centre, says of this weather picture: 'You can get narrow belts of strong wind around the centre of a developing low, in this case accentuated by the edge of the Gulf Stream.'

148

Altogether, I spent about 14 days in the Gulf Stream. It is impossible to tell with any precision how much foul current I had to contend with—somewhere between 230 and 330 nautical miles is the best estimate I can make. I probably stayed too far south for too long. But what finally killed my chances of winning the *Jester* Trophy was a shallow low that came through the leaders of the *Jester* fleet on June 26. Ahead and to the North of me, *Third Turtle* and *Spaniel* were on the north-west corner of the low, enjoying easterlies and north-easterlies. I was on the southern edge of it, feeling the full force of it from the west. While *Third Turtle* and *Spaniel* roared away with the wind behind them, *FT* was hove to for a total of 12 hours. By the time the storm had passed over me, they were both more than $2\frac{1}{2}$ days ahead. Meanwhile, to the North, the storm was doing severe damage to Clare Francis. Her self-steering, which had been threatening to break for nearly two weeks, finally split in two. Only her remarkable courage succeeded in bringing *Robertson's Golly* the remaining 800 miles to Newport. This gale, almost as much as that of June 14, decided the finishing order of the *Jester* fleet. *Third Turtle* used the north-easterly winds to pass *Spaniel* for the last time and went on to win the *Jester* class by the tiny margin of three hours. At its height, *FT* came closer to being overwhelmed by the ocean than at any time in the three seasons I sailed her.

June 26: Last night, after one of the loveliest day's sailing I have had, the weather turns nasty. First, the wind increases to force seven, and I spend two hours on the foredeck making one sail-change after another. When I finally turn in, I feel sick—too much chocolate during the day. Between 2 and 4 this morning, the wind gradually dies, and I make two more sail changes. Alone at sea, I am the slave of the wind—it is my alarm clock, my nightcap, when it feels cussed, it torments me, in a generous mood it brings *FT* and me to life.

By 4 a.m., the wind has died altogether. I take the sails down and catch two hours sleep. At 6, I am up again getting under way under cutter rig. But I am so tired that it takes me $2\frac{1}{2}$ hours to get her under way and settled, to check my position, to pump out the bilges.

At 8.30 a.m., I go back to sleep, leaving the wind alarm set on 35 knots. It wakes me at 9.45. The wind is much stronger, I hand the yankee jib, take more rolls in the main. But the wind is still freshening, I am fearful of tearing the staysail, my most hard-worked sail. I go forward to the sail locker and dig out the storm jib, a sail I have not used since the Round Britain Race.

It is all a waste of effort. Over the next hour, the windspeed rises further. To add to a general feeling of despondency, the *Saloniki* of Piraeus passes within 50 yards of me without so much as a wave from her bridgedeck. I try to call her up on my Seavoice VHF radio, but there is no answer. When there is no shipping around, it does not bother me at all if I have no one to talk to. But when other human beings are 50 yards away, I long to hear another human voice, I feel rejected by the officer on the watch. Or perhaps he never saw me. He came horribly close if he did not.

At 10.30, it is all too much for *FT*. The wind is gusting up to 40 knots, *FT* is taking a terrible hammering, only moving 4 knots, and only pointing slightly west of north. I decide to stop and lie a-hull. I roll the mainsail down, secure the boom, take all the sails off the foredeck and stuff them into the sail locker. The seas are already steepening, the glass has fallen rapidly from 1011 to 1005. I lash the helm over, *FT* seems comfortable, but the seas are growing bigger all the time, the crests are beginning to tumble away from them.

I go up on deck, stand on the coachroof, watch *FT* rising and falling to these waves. *FT* sinks into a trough, the top of the great rolling wave that is coming towards me seems to tower above her 46-foot mast. Above, the sky is a leaden grey, low cloud scudding across it. *FT* is lying at 90 degrees to the wind, which is shrieking through the rigging; we are climbing up the back of the wave, the top of it is tumbling over towards us, it engulfs the weather float, then bodily lifts the main hull and we surf sideways before the wave carries on through to the lee float and we are gliding down its face. I have read that in these conditions, it is safer to raise the centreboard, because the moving part of the wave, the bubbling, crashing surge that has just launched us sideways, moves across the top of the water, carrying the top two or three feet of the ocean with it. With centreboard up, so the theory went as I read it in my armchair at home, a multihull will slide sideways with the breaking crest, whereas if her centreboard is down, it will act as a brake, and the wave could then turn her over her lee float.

I raise the centreboard. At 12.15, the heaviest squall I have ever been in hits *FT*. The windspeed meter goes up to 50 knots, the noise of the wind outside rises to a shrill scream. The seas flatten out. For about ten minutes, everything goes horizontal and turns white. Spray and spindrift is taken off the water by the wind, and driven across the top of it in sheets. The huge seas of a few minutes ago have been reduced to a rippling flat surface, cowering in front of the wind.

So often have I wondered what I would do in this situation. I find myself to be totally calm, singing half-remembered pop-songs from my teens over and over again. 'On a day like today, we pass the time away, writing love letters in the sand. . . .' Why that song? I have not heard it for years. But I just keep singing it. At the height of the squall, I go and get the movie-camera, and stick it up through the hatch, I must have a record of what force ten looks like. I check all my capsize equipment—the diving mask, the flippers, the air bottle and the return valve. If *FT* capsizes, I shall try and stay on board, take out the baron log from the bottom of the boat, use the hole that it leaves behind as my air hole. I put together a set of spare clothes, wrap them all up in a black plastic dustbin bag, put it near the air cylinder and the diving equipment. There is no panic, I am just very quietly thinking through what I may have to do, hoping that it will not come to that.

With the squall past, the big seas come back, and for a few brief moments, the sun comes out. I go on deck, watch *FT*'s motion. As the breaking surf picks her up, she is being bodily lifted sideways by it, just as the book said she would be. But her deep-sided floats are digging into the sea, are being pressed right under water. There are three inches of green water over the float before the wave finally passes through and lifts the lee float out again.

In retrospect, I should probably have tried putting the centreboard half down to stop the float digging in so badly. At the time, as I stand on the coachroof, rising to the top of a wave and look in awe around me at miles and miles of breaking white waves, I feel *FT* is comfortable and can cope. I go down below again, and write in my log. 'It feels much safer down here than on deck.' I stay below, watch her handling the seas for a while, watch the wind slowly decrease to 40 knots. 'If these waves start to curl, they will turn me over,' I tell myself. But the wind is slowly subsiding, the waves are no longer getting steeper, I cannot summon up the energy to go back on deck again. 'It feels much safer below.' Instead, I start finding things to do. I have an all-over wash. I change my clothes. I even dart up on deck with no clothes on under my oilskins to try and take a sunsight—a pointless exercise in these seas. At 2.30 p.m., less than two hours after the squall, I lie down and fall asleep.

June 26, 1830: I have been asleep all afternoon, with just one brief wake-up to check things out. I have decided not to set off again until the wind speed falls below 25 knots—a not particularly subtle excuse for staying in my sleeping bag. At 6.30 p.m., I wake up and look at the windspeed meter. It is reading 23 knots. Damn. Why can I not be left alone to sleep? That will mean a hard slog all through the night. After ten minutes, I drag myself out of my sleeping bag, put my feet ginerly into the cold water that is swilling above the floorboards, rub some water into my eyes to remove the sleep and the salt. Where is the wind coming from? I look at the Hasler wind vane, dolefully pick up the hand-bearing compass to check the wind's direction. It reads 45 degrees. Forty-five degrees. That cannot be right, that is north-east. I check it again. It *is* north-east. The wind is behind me. It is a dead run to Newport.

Never have I moved so fast on board a boat. Within ten minutes, I am in my oilskins, the mainsail is up, we are heading south-west, the self-steering is attached. After an hour, I even debate with myself whether to put the spinnaker up. But I remember *Gulf Streamer* and her capsize in the aftermath of a gale, and decide to take it easy tonight. The seas are confused, still coming from the west, but beginning to respond to the north-easterly. As darkness falls, I hoist the no. 2 genoa and goosewing it, and leave *FT* for the night, with six rolls in her main, running towards Newport at 8½ knots. The last entry in my log reads: 'The end of an eventful day.'

June 27: By 8.30, I have the small spinnaker up and have shaken all the rolls out of the main. By 11.30, the big red, white and blue spinnaker is up, all 1200 square feet of it. It is a perfect day's sail, sun out, spinnaker drawing, deep blue water, warm wind, the sort of day I dream about during those long winter evenings. At 6.30, I take a sunsight and mark my position on the chart. In the 24 hours since I set off after the storm, I have sailed 201 miles through the water, and have covered 190 miles on the chart. It is the best 24 hours of the race. The contrast with the storm the previous day is total.

It did not last, of course. Nothing ever does at sea. By the middle of the next night, the spinnaker was down—that was the only time it was used during the whole race. On June 28 and 29, I got into some fierce Gulf Stream currents, and was driven back about 60 miles. On the afternoon of June 30, I finally cleared the Gulf Stream. In the middle of the night, the fog came in.

EPILOGUE

FT came third in the *Jester* class. Less than three hours later, Wally Greene in *Friends* crossed the line. If I had not pressed on across the Nantucket Shoals during my last night at sea, if I had not left her sailing through the night when I finally cleared the shoals, *FT* would only have been fourth. That is how close it was at the very end.

FT went to the starting line at Plymouth a good enough boat to win the *Jester* Trophy. She was beaten because I made too many mistakes. If I ever do the race again, I shall do almost everything as I did it in 1976. But there will be one or two changes. I will not make the same mistakes twice. Here are the things I would do differently:

1 **Training:** I went to the starting line fitter than I have ever been in my adult life. Yet throughout the first week, I was fighting seasickness, trying to adjust my body to the thoroughly unsocial hours of life at sea, waiting for the cuts on my hands to become resistant to continuous contact with salt water. I would not enter the race again unless I was sure that I could spend a minimum of two months before the start doing nothing but sail. It is easy to say that, not so easy to treat one's family and one's job as one would have to in order to do it. But winning the OSTAR is now as difficult as winning a gold medal at the Olympics. To beat the Tabarlys of this world, you have to behave like the professionals that they are. Had I done it this time, I would have been sea-fit at the start. And I would have discovered the kind of irritating equipment failure that I experienced with the hurricane lamp: keeping that lamp alight cost me more hours of sleep than I care to think about.

2 **Self-steering:** The decision never to steer the boat myself was an error. Having taken it before the start, it was very easy once out on the ocean to justify it to myself. *FT* lost a lot of ground through 'weaving', far more than she would have if I had disciplined myself to steer five or six hours a day. In addition, when close-hauled, I could steer *FT* between five and

ten degrees closer to the wind than the self-steering could, depending on the size of the sea. Since I was close-hauled for 21 out of 27 days, six hours a day would have greatly improved my overall performance, though possibly at the cost of dangerously over-exhausting myself.

3 **Strategy:** I spent hours poring over the chart table, many of them wasted hours. In the event, I made two serious strategic errors. It was a mistake to go south on June 14; and it was an error to stay in the Gulf Stream towards the end of the race rather than to ease myself north in search of the Labrador Current. There were good reasons at the time for taking both decisions. But I now know, with the benefit of hindsight, that I would have done better to do differently. If I were doing the race again, I would avoid both the Azores route and the Great Circle. Both commit you too far one way or the other, and both have serious built-in risks. The Azores route is too far, and the risk of flat calms is too great. The Great Circle is too close to the bad weather. I would also try and keep a more open mind on where I was going once out at sea, and not be quite so keen to settle on a strategy and stick to it. Having said all that, I have no doubt at all that one day, the race will be won by boats on the Azores and Great Circle routes. The element of luck in this race will always be there.

4 **Target time:** I was quite right to set myself a target time. It provides a vital benchmark as you go across. My mistake was to make my target 28 days. This was far too generous. In the event, *Third Turtle* won the *Jester* class in 24 days 20½ hours, and *FT* was 2⅓ days behind her. Mike Birch feels that with more clement weather, he could have got *Third Turtle* to Newport even faster.

Target-setting for this race is never going to be easy. But if I were entering the large class for the next race (under 46-foot waterline), I would aim at 18 days. That is two days faster than Alain Colas's record, set in the 1972 race, and even that might not be fast enough. The new generation of multihulls, and the rapid development of singlehanded sailing techniques and equipment, make a 15-day OSTAR by no means an impossibility. The new size limit on the top class will in my view lead to faster not slower crossings, as skippers and designers concentrate on getting the best out of a 46-foot waterline instead of going for size.

5 **Equipment:** One of the reasons I stayed in the Gulf Stream was to avoid the icebergs and the fog. A decision deliberately to sail singlehanded through icebergs is a very personal one—one that I would never take. The fog, on the other hand, is inescapable. You are bound, at some point, to hit it, and when you hit it you will be surrounded by fishing boats on the Grand Banks and the Georges Bank. I would go to enormous lengths to make myself more visible and more audible in the fog. You have to plan on being in it for at least a week.

Will I ever do the OSTAR again? When I arrived in Newport, I said definitely not. I had loved the race and the sail. But the whole OSTAR effort had taken too great a toll of my life for too long a time, the risks were greater than I felt a man with a family had a right to expose himself to. Now, eight months later, I am not so sure. Writing this book has been a true catharsis for me. It has reminded me of feelings and emotions that I had forgotten, and as I have come to each new chapter, so my attitude towards the race has changed with the mood of the time I have been writing about.

Maybe in ten, fifteen, twenty years, when the children are no longer children, and I would not be putting our family at risk? But that is so far away that to think about it is meaningless, to dream about it an illusion.

And yet . . . To win the OSTAR is still for me the ultimate challenge that a yachtsman can face. Whether or not I face it again, the *FT* project and the 1976 OSTAR will remain a milestone in my life. The experience was an overwhelming one, and my life is the richer for having done it.

APPENDIX

I

WHY MULTIHULLS?

For most of the 1974 Round Britain Race, four multihulls were competing closely with each other for the first four places. They were *British Oxygen*, a 70-foot Macalpine-Downie catamaran; *Three Cheers* and *Gulf Streamer*, both trimarans from the Dick Newick stable, respectively 46 feet and 60 feet overall; and *Triple Arrow*, a 49-foot Simpson-Wild trimaran. All four have since either capsized or broken up, and two of their skippers are dead.

I am writing this appendix for two reasons—partly, because I wish to share as widely as possible whatever experience I have gained over three seasons with *FT*; partly, because I am fed up with listening to the opinions of two kinds of people about multihulls. On the one hand are the flat-earth monohullers, who have never set foot on board a multihull but will argue until the yacht club bar falls asleep that they are unsafe. On the other hand are the committed multihull fraternity, who approach the subject as apostles of a new religion. Every capsize is a special case to be explained away as untypical; every structural failure is all the fault of some welder in a garage who did not do his job properly.

My own position is, I hope, somewhere near the rational centre between these two extremes. I became involved with multihulls because I wanted to win a specific race, which was and remains open to both monohulls and multihulls. I believed then, and I believe even more strongly now, that a multihull will outsail a monohull of the same size over any course in the world. I did not order a multihull because of some Pauline conversion to them. Frankly, I regard the whole monohull-multihull argument as irrelevant. Multihulls are an exciting breakthrough in the search for speed on the water. They are here to stay. What is badly needed is some dispassionate research into the whole subject of multihull design and safety in order that they can be made as safe as possible for those who choose to sail them.

Why sail them at all? Here, for me, are the reasons why, and the purposes for which they are suitable:

1 **Open racing:** If you want to win either the OSTAR or the Round Britain Race, you need a multihull. True, monohulls won two of the three classes in the 1976 OSTAR. But in the *Jester* class, where

multihulls ought to have had less of an advantage over monos, they
filled three of the first four places.

2 **Fast cruising**: If speed matters to you, then you will get there
quicker in a multihull. Some families who sail multihulls do so because
the period between ports is considerably diminished, and children do
not have so much time to get bored. Others, myself included, find the
sensation of speed at sea offers an exhilaration all of its own.

3 **Comfort**: Living upright at sea all the time is either to or against
your taste. Most yachtsmen who have spent a lifetime at 60 degrees
wrestling with a gimballed stove look on the idea of being level all the
time as a bit sissy. On the whole, their wives and children take the
opposite view.

4 **Cost**: As a general rule, you get more berths per pound spent on a
cruising multihull than on a monohull. This is especially true of
cruising catamarans where the floats are usually used for accommoda-
tion. Syndicate sailing, or getting the family on the water, is therefore
cheaper.

That is by no means an exclusive list. But for most multihullers, the
initial decision to get involved will have been taken for at least two of
these reasons.

Now comes the rub. What *are* the risks? I offer here what seem to
me to be the main considerations that anyone ordering a multihull
should take into account:

1 **The state of the art**: When I first ordered *FT*, I imagined the
state of the art to be far further advanced than it is. I learned the
hard way that modern racing multihulls are at a painfully early stage
of development. If you order a racing multihull, you are taking the
same kind of risk, and for the same kind of reason, that was taken by
the early aviators. Already, two leading multihull designers have lost
their lives sailing their own designs—Hedley Nicol in Australia and
Arthur Piver in America. The list of first-class seamen who have
drowned is a lengthening one. The multihull designer, asked to
design a racing machine, is trying to reconcile two mutually contra-
dictory priorities—lightness and strength. It is exactly the same
conundrum that faces aircraft designers. In the early days of aircraft,
before the aircraft manufacturers were awarded massive government
research contracts and had built testbeds in which to test their
designs to destruction, aircraft fell out of the sky because the designers
got their sums wrong, and test pilots lost their lives. The same is
happening with racing multihulls. Since there is not the slightest
prospect of governments funding research into multihull design, we
are going to have to fall back on the well-tried testing method used
ever since human beings first put to sea—suck it and see.

2 **Cruising multihulls:** I have deliberately confined the above paragraph to the racing machines—the *British Oxygens*, the *FT*s, the *Triple Arrows*. The decision to buy one of the many cruising multihulls on the market is of a quite different order of risk. In purely *structural* terms, most cruising multihulls are built well within known weight-to-strength safety ratios. Most of them are undercanvassed and over-engineered, so that there is a large safety factor built into their design.

3 **Capsize:** There is no such thing as an uncapsizeable multihull. The 1976 season—the worst multihulls have ever had—has put paid to that myth for ever. There is no such thing as an uncapsizeable monohull either. But the difference is that when a monohull is either knocked down or turns through 360 degrees, it more often than not comes back upright again without sinking. When a multihull capsizes, it *always* stays upside down.

Most families who go cruising do not go out in weather that might cause a capsize. So for coastal cruising, or the odd dash across the English Channel, there is no need for the capsize factor to weigh too heavily on the mind of somebody considering buying a multihull. But to ignore the capsize factor would be just as foolish as to overstate it. The further from port you go, the greater the risk of encountering conditions in which a multihull *might*, under an unlucky combination of circumstances, capsize, before you can make it back to safety. Similarly, the harder it is blowing, the greater the risk that a mistake will be made—a sheet will snag, a wheel will jam, a spinnaker will refuse to come down—and a multihull will be turned over by the wind.

Having said that, let me qualify it further. Multihulls when they capsize continue to float upside down. There is therefore a reasonable chance that some or all members of the crew will survive until rescued. The list of seasoned and experienced multihullers who have capsized and lived to tell the tale is very long—Derek Kelsall, Nick Keig, Phil Weld, Bill Howell, Robin Musters, Tom Follett, Mike Butterfield, to name just a few. If you can survive the first minute of a capsize—and that is the really dangerous time—and if you have planned properly against the risk of it, and if the water is warm enough, your chances of survival are very high.

This does *not*—as has often been argued by the multihull apostles—make multihulls 'safer than monohulls' (which, if they are going to sink, make a proper job of it and go all the way to the bottom). It provides a balancing factor against the risk of capsize for anyone trying to decide whether he wants to take himself and/or his family, out sailing in one.

My choice of a tri over a cat for single-handed racing has been mentioned on page 39.

Conclusion: My own attitude to multihulls is agnostic. If I ever enter either the Round Britain or the OSTAR again, I would expect it to be in a multihull, because if I enter a race, I do so to win it. For coastal cruising with the family, I would happily take any of the well-tried production multihulls. For ocean passage-making, I would turn to a monohull. And if I live to fulfil my retirement dream of sailing very slowly round the world with Elizabeth, it will be in a large, comfortable, beamy boat with a powerful engine, at least two masts with not too much canvas on either of them and a solid keel underneath.

II

THE CHANGES TO *FT*

Before writing this section of the appendix, one word of caution. I am neither an engineer nor a yacht designer. My sole qualification to write about multihull design and construction is the experience gained in five seasons of multihull sailing—two in an Iroquois catamaran and three in *FT*. I therefore write as a customer who holds opinions about his boats in the same way as most car drivers hold opinions about their cars.

I shall describe in detail all the significant alterations we made to *FT* during the winter of 1974–75. Most of these changes were made with Derek Kelsall's encouragement and help, and to his designs. Throughout the *FT* project, Derek has been generous with his time and with his advice. By the time *FT* went to the starting line of the OSTAR, she was a fine and seaworthy boat. And she was undoubtedly fast enough to win the *Jester* Trophy. I could have asked for no more.

A. THE OLD BEAMS

I have described in Chapter Two (p. 42) how and why the type of aluminium alloy beam used on *FT* was chosen. Not to put too fine a point on it, it was *faute de mieux*. At the time, there were shortages throughout British industry, and we could not get the round aluminium alloy tubes that were originally specified.

The top half of Figure 13 shows the old beams, and includes a detailed section showing how they were made (section 'xx'). The beams were formed of a flat piece of $\frac{1}{4}$-inch aluminium—$8\frac{1}{2}$ inches wide for the top beam and 6 inches for the bottom, to which were glued and bolted two 3-inch angle sections, also of $\frac{1}{4}$-inch thickness. The type of aluminium alloy used was H30 WP.

The beams were joined at the centre by aluminium plates, so that to all intents and purposes, they formed a continuous whole from one float through the hull to the other.

The forward beam configuration was attached to the main hull by

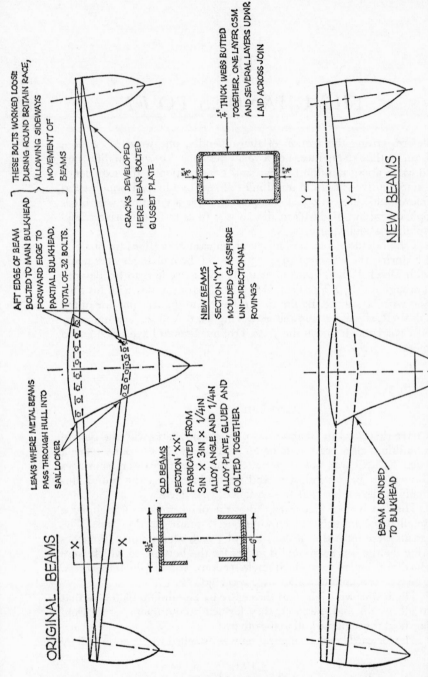

13 The old and new beams.

sets of four half-inch bolts in eight separate places. The forward edge of both the top and bottom beam was bolted to a pair of partial bulkheads fitted for that specific purpose. The aft edge was bolted into the main bulkhead, with the heads of the bolts visible in the main cabin, but glassed over to prevent leaks.

The aft beam configuration was only bolted to the boat on its forward edge—onto the bulkhead that divided the cockpit in half.

At the outboard ends, the beams were bolted together by eight half-inch bolts (four on either side), and were further held together by two gusset plates (one on either side) (see Fig. 14 and plate 10). The bottom beam was then bolted into the deck of the float (forward), and the bridge (aft) by a total of six bolts.

OLD BEAMS
DETAIL OF FORWARD BEAM
ATTACHMENT TO FLOAT

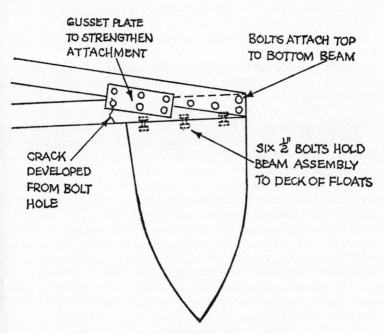

14 Old beams: detail of forward beam attachment to float.

In terms of both weight and strength, this beam configuration should have been entirely adequate. The Wolfson unit study states: 'It is not considered that the original aluminium alloy struts were wrong in concept as crossbeams for *FT*, or were built generally too light.' In practice, however, they did not work:

1 **Early problems:** From the very first sail, it was clear that the lower forward beam was too near the water, so that when *FT* pitched, it slammed into waves, sending shocks through the rest of the boat. We tried to remedy this by fitting fairings onto the forward edge of the beam. This helped only marginally. We also found that the lower beams, because they were channel section with the channel facing upwards, were almost permanently full of water. We therefore covered these with a thin aluminium sheet 'roof', that was riveted into the sides of the beam.

2 **The lifting rear beam:** Because the rear beam did not have a partial bulkhead behind it, it was only bolted to the boat at its forward edge. After several months hard sailing, the aft edge started to lift away from the deck, mainly, I believe, as a result of loads transmitted from the mast through the cap and inner shrouds to the aft end of the float. These loads tended to lift the stern of the float, which in turn twisted the beam. The problem was solved by tying the back of the top beam to the back of the bottom one by four stainless steel straps.

3 **The loosening bolts:** The basic theory of a two-beam structure is that the top beam will be in compression, and the bottom one in tension when upward pressure is put on the float from the heeling action of the boat. The further apart the beams are at the point where they penetrate the hull, the 'stiffer' is the whole configuration.

The lateral forces operating through *FT*'s beams were so great that the bolts holding them to the bulkheads—made of 12 mm plywood glassed on both sides—began to work loose. Once this process had started, there was no way of stopping it. As the bolts worked loose, the holes in the bulkheads were enlarged, and the movement of the beams increased, so further enlarging the holes.

4 **The cracked beams:** The two forward beams cracked away from one of the bolts holding the gusset plate in place at the outboard end of the beams (Fig. 14). The aft beam cracked away from one of the rivet holes that was holding the aluminium sheet 'roof' in place to prevent the beam filling with water. In the opinion of the Wolfson unit, these holes had been drilled too close to the edges of the aluminium angle sections. The locations of these holes could, in the opinion of the Wolfson unit, have resulted in stress concentrations of $3\frac{1}{2}$ times the average which would normally occur at that point in

the structure. The Wolfson unit also expressed concern at the use of bolting as a means of joining the beams to each other at the outboard ends. 'The success of bolting as a method of joining structural members relies on a good fit of the bolt in a hole, with tolerances between them of the order of 0·001 of an inch. Such tolerances cannot normally be achieved with hand held drills unless a reamer tool is also used.'

The position of the crack on the three beams that went was exactly the same—on the aft edge of the lower beam, roughly three inches inboard of the float. On the final stretch of our sail into Lowestoft, when we knew we had a cracked beam, I was able to watch the crack working. Every time *FT* heeled over, the crack opened up; as she lifted her float from the water, it closed again.

A combination of four sets of forces were operating on this section of the beam:

(i) The normal tension stresses for which the beam was designed.
(ii) An upward thrust, as the wind sank the float into the water, and the buoyancy of the float began to operate.
(iii) A twisting moment, partly caused by the deep shape of the float acting like a centreboard; partly caused by the shock loads when a trimaran falls off a wave, and lands on the side of its float.
(iv) The location of the cap shroud and the inner shroud bridle on the inboard side of the float transmitted a similar twisting moment to the windward float, which accepted loads transmitted from the mast and sailplan.

5 **Conclusion:** The Wolfson study concluded that the basic concept of the beams had been sound; but that the final detailing—in particular the location of holes that were drilled after the boat had been launched—had weakened the structure. The study also felt that the problem of getting a really good fit when using bolts as fasteners was 'further complicated at the connection of the struts to the main hull due to the lower bearing strength of the ply bulkhead to which the struts were attached when compared with aluminium.'

My own conclusion is rather more radical. I believe that attempts to join metal to glass fibre at points where vast loads are being transmitted from one material to the other are doomed to failure. This is not because there is anything inherently wrong with metal—if an aircraft wing can be made of metal, then so can a multihull beam. It is born of a fundamental distrust of the known state of the art of joining metal to glass fibre; and of a dislike of certain of the qualities of metal beams as they have turned out in practice:

(i) The normal method of bonding a round tubular beam to glass is to apply resin to the beams and then to bond the glass fibre to the resin. There have been a number of cases of this bond breaking loose, usually without warning.

(ii) Most boatyards subcontract their welding to outside jobshops. Quality control of the welding is therefore difficult. The loss of *Johnwillie* was put down by John Westell to a faulty weld.

(iii) The record of failures in metal beams is a poor one. I have detailed here what happened to *FT*'s and why. During the 1976 OSTAR, *British Oxygen*, *Quest*, *Croda Way*, *Cap 33* and *Spirit of Surprise* all had varying degrees of trouble with metal beams. Only *Quest* and *Cap 33* reached the finishing line.

(iv) If a metal beam is going to fatigue, it does so without warning. If a glass fibre beam is weakening, it does so in visible and audible stages. Glass fibre beams, therefore, contain their own built in warning device.

Derek Kelsall will argue at the end of this appendix that I am going far too far in my condemnation of metal in multihulls. My judgement is obviously coloured by my experience with *FT*. I can only say that if I were ordering a new boat, nothing would induce me to accept metal beams. That is the judgement of a customer, not of a scientist.

B. THE NEW BEAMS

FT's new beams were built by Derek Kelsall at Sandwich. He delivered them by road to St Helens, where they were fitted by Attrill and Sons boatyard. From the moment they were fitted, they never failed in any way whatever. The following qualities also made them preferable for my purposes (See Fig. 13):

1 The forward beam was fitted high above the water. Although there were some seas that still broke into the beams, the problem of the lower beam hitting the water was 90 per cent cured. Had we had more time to design and test these beams, they could have been made of a curved wing-like shape which would have cleared the water altogether.

2 The bond between the main hull and the beam was a perfect one. There were therefore no leaks of water into the sail locker through the join between the beam and the hull.

3 I found glass fibre to be an easier material to work with, and easier to repair.

4 A hollow glass fibre beam contains an added element of safety. In potential capsize conditions it acts as additional buoyancy if the float should be pressed underwater. If the boat *does* capsize, and if the beams are watertight, they will cause the boat to float higher when inverted.

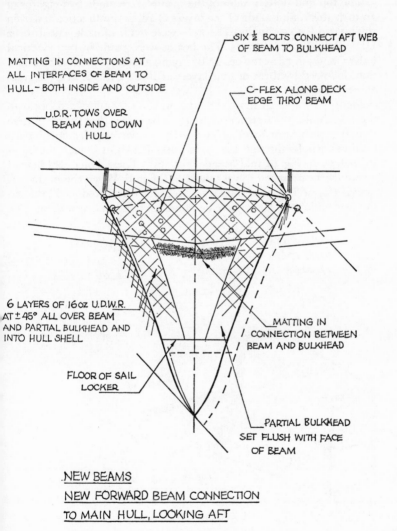

SIX ½ BOLTS CONNECT AFT WEB OF BEAM TO BULKHEAD

MATTING IN CONNECTIONS AT ALL INTERFACES OF BEAM TO HULL – BOTH INSIDE AND OUTSIDE

C-FLEX ALONG DECK EDGE THRO' BEAM

U.D.R. TOWS OVER BEAM AND DOWN HULL

6 LAYERS OF 16oz U.D.W.R. AT ± 45° ALL OVER BEAM AND PARTIAL BULKHEAD AND INTO HULL SHELL

MATTING IN CONNECTION BETWEEN BEAM AND BULKHEAD

FLOOR OF SAIL LOCKER

PARTIAL BULKHEAD SET FLUSH WITH FACE OF BEAM

NEW BEAMS
NEW FORWARD BEAM CONNECTION TO MAIN HULL, LOOKING AFT

15 New beams: new forward beam connection to main hull.

Figure 13 shows details of the construction of the beams. They are of an absolutely basic design, with no attention paid either to aesthetics or windage (the forward beam was originally fitted with a light fairing, but this broke off almost immediately, and was not replaced).

The top and bottom sides of the beams were made five-eighths of an inch thick, and made of ten layers of 16 oz unidirectional woven roving laid longitudinally. The webs were made of six layers of 16 oz UDWR laid at 45 degrees. The beams were made in two identical halves, and joined at the centre by laying a layer of $1\frac{1}{2}$ oz chopstrand mat, followed by three or four layers of 16 oz UDWR at 45 degrees across the join.

Figures 15 and 16 show the attachment of the forward beam to the main hull. My instructions were to be safe rather than sorry, so that the glass fibre bonding of the beams was supplemented by a total of 12 bolts through the main bulkhead—just in case the bond started to spring in mid-ocean (Fig. 15). These bolts also helped locate the beam when it was joined to the hull. When the beam was married up to the main bulkhead, wet mat was introduced between the two surfaces to try and create an initial bond between them. The

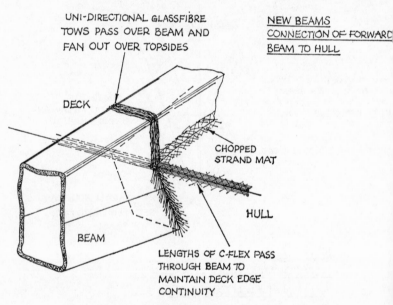

16 New beams: connection of forward beam to hull.

forward edge of the beam sat on a partial bulkhead, and layers of 16 oz were laid across beam and bulkhead. Then at every point where the beam formed a corner with the hull, chopstrand mat was pressed onto both surfaces.

On the outside surface of the hull, tows of unidirectional roving were wetted through, passed over the beam and fanned out over the outer hull. (Fig. 16). Along the deck edge, lengths of C-flex were pushed through holes in the beam to prevent any tendency for the deck either to pull apart or to push together.

Out at the floats, the same belt and braces policy was used. The forward float attachment, which is subject to far heavier shock loads than the aft one, was made with two half-inch plywood bulkheads (Fig. 17). For added strength, each of the forward bulkheads had stainless steel straps bolted across it.

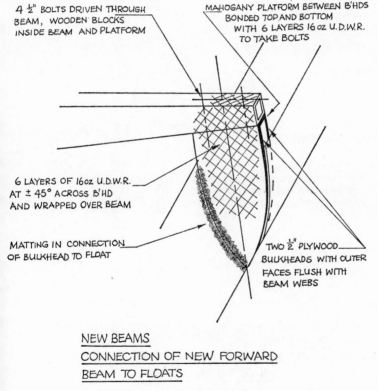

4 ½" BOLTS DRIVEN THROUGH BEAM, WOODEN BLOCKS INSIDE BEAM AND PLATFORM

MAHOGANY PLATFORM BETWEEN B'HDS BONDED TOP AND BOTTOM WITH 6 LAYERS 16 oz U.D.W.R. TO TAKE BOLTS

6 LAYERS OF 16oz U.D.W.R. AT ± 45° ACROSS B'HD AND WRAPPED OVER BEAM

MATTING IN CONNECTION OF BULKHEAD TO FLOAT

TWO ½" PLYWOOD BULKHEADS WITH OUTER FACES FLUSH WITH BEAM WEBS

NEW BEAMS
CONNECTION OF NEW FORWARD
BEAM TO FLOATS

17 New beams: connection of new forward beam to floats.

Between the tops of these two bulkheads, a mahogany platform was fitted, on which the beam was to sit. The whole bulkhead and platform assembly was then glassed together with six layers of 16-oz UDWR. During construction of the beams, wooden blocks had been located inside the beams, and four half-inch bolts were now driven right through the beams and through the platform, both to locate the float and as a failsafe should the fibre glass bond break. Just before the beam and the platform were married together, $1\frac{1}{2}$ oz of wet chopstrand mat was laid between them to provide an initial bond.

The rest of the process consisted of wrapping six layers of UDWR over the beam and onto the bulkheads, to provide one of the strongest —and heaviest—beam-to-float connections that has ever graced a racing multihull.

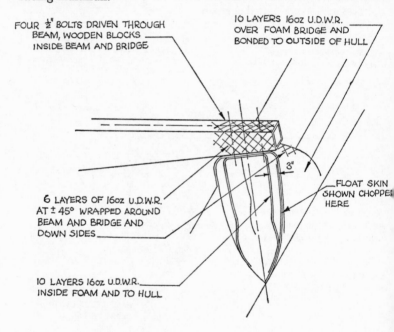

FOUR $\frac{1}{2}$" BOLTS DRIVEN THROUGH BEAM, WOODEN BLOCKS INSIDE BEAM AND BRIDGE

10 LAYERS 16oz U.D.W.R. OVER FOAM BRIDGE AND BONDED TO OUTSIDE OF HULL

6 LAYERS OF 16oz U.D.W.R. AT ± 45° WRAPPED AROUND BEAM AND BRIDGE AND DOWN SIDES

10 LAYERS 16oz U.D.W.R. INSIDE FOAM AND TO HULL

3"

FLOAT SKIN SHOWN CHOPPE HERE

NEW BEAMS
AFT BEAM CONNECTION TO FLOATS
BRIDGE ARRANGEMENT

18 New beams: aft beam connection to floats, bridge arrangement.

One final problem emerged when the whole assembly was in place. We found that because of the bending qualities of the bulkheads, there was insufficient forward and aft rigidity. We therefore added wooden angles on either side of the beam, and glassed them in place —and then used the top surface of the forward ones as a spray deflector.

The rear beams were attached to the existing platform, which was strengthened by adding six layers of UDWR and three of 1½-inch CSM onto its inside and down into the hull (Fig. 18). Once again, the beam was bolted onto the platform being wrapped around with glass fibre.

I conclude this section by quoting direct from the Wolfson study of these beams:

Calculations on the GRP beams are based on the pessimistic assumption that in all loading cases, the forward beam carries all the load.

The highest stresses in the beams are calculated to occur with the loading case of a dynamic upwards force at the float. The results of these calculations indicate:

2nd moment of area, I, for beam at hull = 503 in^4.

The above calculation makes due allowance for fibre orientation in the beam and a pessimistic estimate has been taken for the thickness of the beams with the lay-up specified.

Stresses in beam flanges at still water capsize = 10,300 lbf/in^2

Maximum stresses in beam flanges from dynamic loading = 20,600 lbf/in^2

Ultimate static strength of GRP flanges, minimum figure = 60,000 lbf/in^2

Maximum allowable fluctuating stress in GRP flanges to give fatigue life of 10^5 cycles = 36,000 lbf/in^2

True safety factor = maximum allowable stress to give fatigue life of
$$\frac{10^5 \text{ cycles}}{\text{Maximum calculable stress}} = \frac{36,000}{20,600} = 1 \cdot 75$$

Similar strength checks were conducted for the shear strength of the beams and for the following loading cases:
Rigging loads;
Athwart ships thrust on leeward float;
Longitudinal thrust from burying leeward float.

The Wolfson unit finally compared the strength of the new GRP beams with the old aluminium alloy ones in still water capsize conditions. They calculated that average stresses in the lower strut at still water capsize would have been 6,000 lbf/in²; and that the stress point at which the beam would have yielded with permanent deformation was 37,000 lbf/in².

The factor of ultimate strength over average stresses was calculated as:

$$\text{For the aluminium struts factor} = \frac{37,000}{6,000} = 6 \cdot 1$$

$$\text{For the GRP beams} = \frac{60,000}{10,300} = 5 \cdot 8$$

The Wolfson report concluded:

'The GRP beams are almost as strong as the struts for an overload case and the struts showed no sign of this kind of failure. Because of the lack of stress concentrations in the GRP beams and the materials' good fatigue properties, the beams will be superior in resisting the type of loading which caused the failure of the aluminium struts.'

C. RUDDERS

'Rudders,' John Westell muttered to me in Cork as I surveyed my broken one, 'are a multihull problem.'

FT's rudder (Fig. 19) broke three times during the 1974 season. On each occasion, the reason for the breakage was the same—excessive loading placed on the steering during fast reaching and running conditions.

FT's original rudder was a large and heavy object, which, after our initial accident off Ostend, was made even larger and heavier. By contrast, *Three Legs of Mann*, which Nick Keig has pushed up to 24 knots (against *FT*'s maximum safe speed of 16 knots), has a relatively light and flimsy rudder, which has never caused any trouble.

Why, then, the problems with *FT*? The reason, I believe, lies in some of the extreme points of *FT*'s design. Because the only measurement that mattered for the OSTAR *Jester* class was that the waterline length (LWL) of the main hull should be under 28 feet, as much power as piled on top of this waterline as possible. The floats were 34' 10" long—against 33' 8" for the main hull. The beam was 26 feet —almost as long as her LWL. The mast was 47 feet, carrying an extreme high-aspect-ratio rig.

Imagine now what happens when the wind is after of the beam, usually somewhere on the quarter, a gust hits the boat, and the lee float starts to bury its nose in the wave ahead of it prior to climbing on top of it into a surfing position. First, the float takes a gradually increasing flotation load as it is pressed underwater—and *FT*'s floats had the great mass of their buoyancy in the bows. Secondly, the real waterline length of the float increases to very nearly 35 feet. Thirdly, because the bows of *FT*'s floats protruded an inch or two in front of the bows of the main hull, and because there was about a three-foot overhang on the bows of the main hull, *the bow of the float at the waterline is about three feet ahead of the bow of the main hull at the waterline.*

In an important sense, therefore, the bow of the float under these circumstances has taken over the directional stability of the boat. The rudder is being asked to steer an object which is 13 feet to one side of it and 35 feet ahead of it. This imposes great strain on the rudder. What in practice the rudder does is to steer the main hull, which in turn takes the float with it.

On a 'normal' trimaran, where the main hull is much longer than

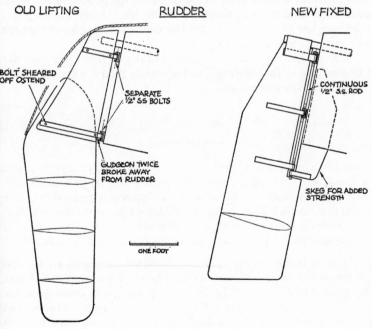

OLD LIFTING   <u>RUDDER</u>   NEW FIXED

BOLT SHEARED OFF OSTEND

SEPARATE ½" SS BOLTS

GUDGEON TWICE BROKE AWAY FROM RUDDER

CONTINUOUS ½" S.S. ROD

SKEG FOR ADDED STRENGTH

ONE FOOT

19 Rudder: old lifting and new fixed.

the floats, this is no problem. But on *FT* the float has too much control of directional stability, and the main hull not enough. The strains on the rudder therefore increase out of all proportion to the 'normal' strains associated with trimarans.

We solved the problem in three ways:

1 I knew during the winter of 1974–75 that, sailing singlehanded, I would never press *FT* as hard as we had in the summer of 1974. We therefore substantially reduced the size of the rudder, accepting that this would mean broaching under some circumstances where we would not have to before. The underwater length of the blade came down from 3′ 6″ to 2′ 8″.

2 We switched to a fixed rudder, and accepted the risk that I would hit some underwater object in mid-Atlantic and lose the blade entirely. The fixed rudder was made of African mahogany, laminated in vertical strips, and sheathed with two laminates of $1\frac{1}{2}$-oz chopstrand mat, with a maximum thickness of $2\frac{1}{2}$ inches.

3 To prevent the tendency for the blade to bend when under pressure, a strong skeg was fitted through the bottom of the transom. This provided a third attachment point for the rudder to the boat, about a third of the way down the blade. The whole assembly was held together by a half-inch stainless steel rod that passed through all three gudgeons and pintles.

We never had any further trouble from the rudder. Only once did I lose control of the steering—and it was as good a warning as any that I had too much sail up.

D. SAIL PLAN

I was much influenced in deciding on *FT*'s final sail plan by a picture of *Three Cheers* and *Gulf Streamer*, reaching together in the Solent under cutter rig (see Plate 16). I had decided whatever happened to create a new forestay for *FT*, so that we would have a proper cutter configuration with the centre of effort as low as possible.

I considered two principal changes during the 1974–75 winter:

1 Derek Kelsall drew up for me a revised sail plan with six feet cut off the top of the mast; and Terry Pearce of International Yacht Equipment told me that if I accepted this change, he could make me a new mast out of a smaller and lighter section. I rejected this option for two reasons—first, I was fearful of losing *FT*'s outstanding light weather performance. I felt her best chance of winning the OSTAR

was to sail to her strengths—to head south for the light airs, and cream through them. Secondly, so many major changes were being made during the 1974-75 winter that I had neither the money nor the inclination to make any more. On the principle of better the devil you know, I preferred to stick with what I had got. Had 1975 been a heavy weather season, I might have been persuaded to change masts and reduce sail plan in the final winter before the race. If I had done so, the moment of inertia caused by *FT*'s long and heavy mast would have been greatly reduced, and she might have been a far better windward performer in the kinds of winds and seas that she encountered for much of the OSTAR. But that is idle speculation.
2 The solution I actually accepted (Fig. 20) was to retain the existing mast, the big overlapping genoa, the no. 2 genoa and the yankee jib

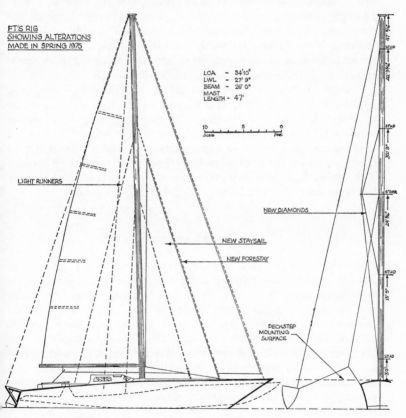

FT'S RIG
SHOWING ALTERATIONS
MADE IN SPRING 1975

LOA — 34'10"
LWL — 27' 9"
BEAM — 26' 0"
MAST
LENGTH - 47'

LIGHT RUNNERS

NEW DIAMONDS

NEW STAYSAIL

NEW FORESTAY

DECKSTEP
MOUNTING
SURFACE

20 *FT*'s rig, showing alterations made in spring 1975.

(not shown on the drawing). The no. 3 genoa was cut back by Peter Dove of Hood to staysail size, and became the most hard-worked sail in my wardrobe. It was permanently rove onto the no. 2 forestay; I put it up for all sail changes so that we kept moving throughout; I used it as part of a cutter rig in winds of force five; and for winds of force six to gale force, I used it as part of a staysail and mainsail combination, thereby bringing the centre of effort aft—away from the bows.

This new rig made an enormous difference to *FT*'s performance. She was still an under-par performer in winds of force six and above. But she could keep going, which in the Round Britain race she could not.

In order to take the loads created by the new staysail, Terry Pearce specified a second set of diamonds, and recommended that I fit light runners from the new forestay position to the beams. By the time I got to the OSTAR start, *FT*'s mast was so well stayed that I believe it would have stayed up even if I had lost a cap shroud or the main forestay. As a by-product of all these changes, I never again encountered the 'panting' problem of the 1974 season.

The moral of this story applies, I believe, to all multihull sail plans. Multihulls are very light, and because of their great beam carry considerable windage to windward. To keep them going into a strong wind and/or a heavy sea, it must be possible to bring the centre of effort down (to reduce the capsize moment) and aft (to minimise the tendency for the headsail to blow the bow off the tops of waves). This means that multihulls must have cutter rig capability; and for heavy weather, they need a staysail-mainsail combination.

E. OTHER CHANGES

1 **Reefing:** Reefing was always a problem with *FT*. We fitted Proctor through-mast roller reefing for 1974. But the cut of the mainsail did not allow us to roll in more than five rolls without the boom starting to sag. On the Round Britain Race, half the sail was fully battened. During the 1974–75 winter, I dispensed with the full battens, and made do with a soft mainsail. This considerably helped the reefing problem, and also allowed a far better set to the main in light airs. In retrospect, I should have gone all the way and switched to slab reefing. The array of poles that I had to roll into the sail to stop the boom sagging; and of blocks and tackles that I used to take tucks out of the leach, made reefing a nightmare. Next time, slab reefing.

2 **Radio reception:** Spencer of Cowes fitted two insulators in my backstay as an aerial for both the ordinary radio, and for short-wave reception using the Brookes and Gatehouse short wave converter. Radio reception had been poor during the Round Britain. From 1975 on, it was excellent, and I was picking up BBC time signals and regular overseas service broadcasts until a few days before the OSTAR finish.

3 **Liferaft position and safety box:** During the Round Britain, we had the liferaft tied to the counter, and our two safety beacons were kept below. I was never happy with this. What would happen if we capsized? We might not reach the liferaft (the stern would probably have floated low); and we might not be able to get at the radios. Attrill's therefore built me a stainless steel cradle on the rear side of the port aft beam into which the liferaft exactly fitted; and they made me a box on the opposite beam into which fitted both the safety radios, some emergency rations, and some survival equipment. Both of these would have been easily accessible with *FT* inverted—provided that I could get out from inside the boat. To do this, I had a small diver's air cylinder with a return valve fitted to it, sufficient to allow me to breathe for 20 minutes. I also carried inside the boat both goggles and divers' flippers.

4 **Pump position:** I moved this from a position on the forward bulkhead above the bunk to the cockpit. This meant that I could pump out the bilge while steering the boat or as part of other on-deck jobs. I also ran a drain hole through to the main bilge from both the sail locker and the aft locker, so that *all* water entering the main hull found its way to the main bilge, and was pumped out from the cockpit. During the transatlantic race, a certain amount of water leaked into the sail locker through the sail locker hatch. In heavy weather, I had to pump out roughly four times a day, and it usually took about ten minutes. I would start to pump when water rose above the level of the main cabin floor.

5 **Spinnaker:** For the 1975 season, I dispensed with a spinnaker pole except when required to use one by a racing rule. When set, each corner of the spinnaker had three lines permanently attached to it—a sheet, a downhaul and a Barber-hauler to the bow of the float. The three lines were all tied to the same snap shackle, so that to attach them only required one hand movement. The spinnaker set beautifully under this arrangement. Gybing was easy. And with the spee-squeezer for hoisting and bringing the sail in, the whole spinnaker operation was delightfully painless. Alas, I only carried a spinnaker for 12 hours on the entire 27-day OSTAR sail.

III

LESSONS FOR MULTIHULL DESIGN

British Oxygen and *Three Cheers* were both lost during the 1976 OSTAR. *Triple Arrow* and *Gulf Streamer* capsized before reaching the start. *Silmaril*, a 31-foot Simpson-Wilde trimaran, flipped on the way home. And a Val class trimaran—a sister ship to *Third Turtle* and *Edith*—turned over when hove-to in a Gulf Stream storm.

Those of us who order and sail multihulls have got to come to terms with the problems of capsize. I offer here a list of requirements that I would insist be built into a multihull at the design stage of any boat—cruiser or racer—that I might order in the future:

1 **Buoyancy:** The yacht must be designed with sufficient buoyancy so that when inverted, she floats high enough to allow a full crew to live on board above the water level. This means incorporating into the design low level bunks or tables or shelves that can double as somewhere to sit or lie when upside down. Phil Weld, who with his crew lived aboard *Gulf Streamer* for several days after her capsize in May 1976, would not have survived if he had not been in warm water at the time (he was in the Gulf Stream), because there was nowhere for him and his crew to spend the first few hours of inversion except in the water.

2 **Escape hatch:** Every multihull must be fitted with an escape hatch, and with some means of getting fresh air below after a capsize. While riding out my one Atlantic storm in *FT*, I decided, in the event of a capsize, to stay inside the boat and to use the Baron log fitting as my air hole. I did not, however, have an escape hatch, and can only guess at where *FT* would have floated. I considered my chances of survival no better than fifty per cent if I had capsized at or near the height of the storm.

3 **Liferaft and beacons:** These must be fitted where they can be reached from an inverted hull. A position for them needs to be thought out at an early stage.

4 **Beams:** Box beams should be divided into watertight compartments, with drain plugs for each. If part of them is damaged for some reason, then the remainder will still remain a flotation chamber.

5 **Floats:** Floats, too, should be divided into watertight compartments. *FT*'s floats were divided into three, which was both safe and

satisfactory. Designers should develop a pumping system for floats that can be operated from the cockpit, and which is permanently installed. All floats leak some of the time, and having to go out and check them in mid-ocean is often unpleasant and sometimes unsafe.
6 **Attachment points:** There should be something to clip onto when on an upturned hull. Multihulls with bridge decks should have several harness clip attachment points permanently fixed to the underside of their hulls.

From this list, it should be obvious that I am not at all sanguine about the possibility of developing 'the uncapsizeable multihull'. If designers concentrate on cure rather than prevention, I have no doubt less lives will be lost. At present, there is a widespread view within the multihull fraternity that soon, a solution will be found to righting a capsized multihull. That is obviously Stage Two of the development process. Stage One is to make sure that a crew can live long enough to attempt a righting—or until a ship passes.

IV

THE FINAL WORD
by Derek Kelsall

For me *FT* began as a little 28-foot LWL racer which I could easily relate, in physical size, design, structure and cost, to numerous previous trimarans I had produced. The overriding lesson to be learnt from this narrative is that sail power and what I term rotational momentum factors are really what determine the scale of such a project, and LWL on its own can be misleading. With *FT* these two factors combined together to overstress both the structure and the budget. In spite of a remarkable race record, *FT* is not amongst my favourite designs.

FT in a number of ways did not go according to plan and, as is often the case, we learnt more from this one design than any other design before or since. I am happy that this information be passed on to anyone who can make use of it.

Rotational momentum factors, the root-cause of my dissatisfaction with the design, exist for every moving vehicle, but they had certainly never proved to be a problem for me in designing yachts. Their significance for *FT* cannot be ignored. A yacht's rotational movement is approximately about the centre of gravity or centre of buoyancy. Buoyancy at a distance from these centres will reduce rotational movement. Weight displaced from the centre of gravity will add to rotational momentum. Comparatively, *FT* had a heavy mast section, a tall rig and long floats on wide overall beam but only a short waterline length on which to sail. I was aware of these factors but underestimated their power, plus I overestimated the effectiveness of the means, in the design, of dealing with the problem. The result is a boat with an unusual tendency to pitch in certain conditions. Practically all of our problems were a direct or indirect result of this tendency to pitch. For example, the forward crossbeam regularly took a dive through the wave top even though it was in a similar relative position to previous designs with no such problem.

To return to the start of the project—David joins a short list of men with whom I have had the pleasure to work to produce one-off racing designs with some considerable success. They are Major-

General Ralph Farrant and *Trifle*, Phil Weld and *Trumpeter*, Nick Keig and *Three Legs of Mann* and Nick Clifton and *Azulao*. In each case the owner had had a considerable influence on the final arrangement. *FT*'s design was the subject of probably the most discussion in this way.

One of David's first requests was that *FT* should not be in any way experimental and that a conservative attitude should be adopted towards structural design. A very sound and sensible way to begin—so where did we go wrong?

FT was aimed at two races—the 1976 OSTAR *Jester* Trophy (under 28-foot LWL) and the Round Britain Race 1974 (under 35-foot LOA). My belief is that such races are usually won or lost during the light-air conditions that do, in an average year, prevail both in the North Atlantic and in our home waters round Britain during June and July. The Round Britain proved to be the exception with very little air for the whole race. The OSTAR had more than its fair share of gales but outside the gales there was a lot of relatively light air. Bill Howell who has taken part in four races, says he had more light air than usual in '76. While sailing the trimaran *Folatre* in the 1964 OSTAR, I was undercanvassed for more than 75 per cent of the time, and in winning the '66 Round Britain Race in *Toria*, it was a spell of superb light-weather sailing that enabled us to get right away from the rest of the fleet. I am still convinced that we were correct to design for the best light-weather performance.

Light-weather performance is primarily achieved with a large and efficient sail area. Accordingly we stepped the tallest mast we felt could be usefully set on a 35-foot long base. We chose 47 feet from deck to mast head. Note, the 35-foot base was the length of the outrigger. In effect, we had turned the usual trimaran arrangement inside out, but in theory that should make little difference. Instead of sailing on a long stabilising main hull and a short lee hull, *FT* had short main hull and long lee hull. In order to retain the submersible outrigger concept the end of the outriggers had to be very fine and just did not counteract the pitching as I had hoped. No doubt, it would have been better to have abandoned the submersible concept and built outriggers with plenty of reserve buoyancy particularly in the ends.

Our very cautious approach put extra weight aloft in mast and rig and extra weight in floats and beams, further increasing the pitching moment. With the advantage of hindsight we were possibly being somewhat naive in not seeing our extremes in sail area etc. as one big experiment.

Pitching has many undesirable side effects. Diving into waves,

183

difficulty in steering, and extra stresses on every part of the boat, to mention just three. The design closely followed that of *Three Legs of Mann*, possibly the most successful trimaran afloat, having won almost every race she entered and set a 340-mile/24-hour single-handed record, and much of *FT*'s gear was either the same or stronger. The rudder is a good example—*FT*'s was much the stronger but the first to give way under the pressure.

The rig would have been adequate in a 40-footer. This we had anticipated, but adding the pitching moment gave the kind of stresses one would expect on a boat 10 feet longer still, something we had not allowed for.

Obviously *FT* was not an easy craft to get the best out of in the rough and I certainly congratulate David on his efforts in this respect. However, anyone who has raced against *FT* in light airs will confirm how well we achieved our aims in this direction and had the general weather been a little kinder a remarkable race record might have become a spectacular one. David's average speed in OSTAR of better than 6 knots is extremely high, so perhaps the picture is not as gloomy as I have painted it and perhaps, to me as designer, the faults loom larger.

David holds the view, understandably in the circumstances, that it is essential to have a full season's practice to prove and test a new design. I hope that I have been able to explain why *FT* was such a troublesome baby and therefore why David's experience is not necessarily typical. *Toria* was raced hard Round Britain within, literally, less than ten hours sailing from launch and suffered no major problems in ten years of hard sailing. *Trifle* was likewise trouble-free—to mention two of my older and well tested designs. This type of development designing is a forward-learning process, without tested models, and sometimes there has to be a step backwards to keep the immediate horizon in perspective.

Structural failure of multihull crossbeams does seem to have occurred more often where metal, usually aluminium, has been used. Each and every case I know of has been slightly different. However, the failure has not been in any of the *basic* members but where members have been joined or subjected to stress concentration for some reason. At the same time there are numerous trimarans sailing with very strongly made aluminium crossbeams and it would be absolutely wrong to suggest that aluminium cannot be used for this purpose.

The necessity to assemble outside in winter, the lack of availability of the tubular sections we wanted and the three-day week all had an influence on *FT*'s beam design and construction. In abandoning the tube design and adopting the channel sections we were forced into a bolting arrangement. The problem here, we now realise, is that where bolts are in shear and subject to alternating loads, extremely fine tolerances are required to prevent any initial movement completely. The average boat builder does not have the experience or the equipment necessary. A hand held drill, on a cold winter's day outside, does not work.

Since *FT* we have done an extensive study of crossbeam structures with the help of Southampton University. In theory the aluminium strut arrangement should be the least weight. However, we have firmly decided that the GRP box beam arrangement is much more practical for the average boat builder. Improved methods of constructing such beams have brought the cost within reason for such one-offs. The curved, faired beams add considerably to the aesthetics of the whole boat.

At the time of designing *FT* we had no yardstick by which to assess the potential performance accurately. We all know that the major factors affecting potential speed are sail area, weight and length. For a period after *FT* we used the IOMR equations but we were only able to do this effectively with the use of our own desk computer. However, we have now derived a very simple formula that will be useful to anyone interested in multihull performance. The formula is based on tank test data on a typical trimaran model but is applicable to cat or tri. We call the formula the K/S performance number (the S comes from John Shuttleworth who contributed the mathematical know-how).

$$\text{K/S performance No.} = \cdot5\sqrt{\frac{\text{SA} \times \text{L}}{\Delta}}$$

where SA = sail area in square feet, L = waterline length in feet, and Δ = displacement in pounds.

This number will accurately compare similar craft in average conditions and can be used as one does a TCF in a rating, i.e. a boat with K/S No. of 1·1 should be ten per cent faster than a boat with a K/S No. of 1·0. Boats like *FT*, *Trifle* and *Three Cheers* have numbers between 0·8 and 1·1. For simple comparison we suggest using foretriangle and triangular mainsail as sail area and LWL and Δ as either measured/weighed or designed. As a rating these would be rated units as defined in a rating rule.

In combination with this we suggest a K/S stability number. This is close to the wind speed, in miles per hour, at which a capsize would occur from a static condition. (Many other factors would affect an actual capsize). The formula is

$$\text{K/S stability No.} = 15 \cdot 8 \sqrt{\frac{\frac{1}{2}Bm \times \Delta}{SA \times CW}}$$

where $\frac{1}{2}Bm$ is distance from centre of yacht to the centre line of the lee hull; Δ is the displacement of the catamaran, but either the displacement or the flotation of the outrigger whichever is least, of the trimaran; CW is the height in feet of the centre of effort of the sails. The K/S stability number should be worked out for different reefed conditions.

These two numbers will give you the best guide there is of how a multihull will sail. A high performance number will give you a fast, lively performance. A low stability number will indicate the need to reef early and possibly a too tender boat. The K/S stability number is likely to be between 30 and 45 for the average racing craft, going up to 55 or more for the heavy cruising trimaran. *FT*'s K/S performance number is 0·87. New extreme designs to be built in the near future will have numbers up to 1·35 or more.

In our design office we find almost daily use for K/S numbers— had we had this data for *FT* we might have been able to set our sights more accurately.

The race for speed is on and with it the increasing likelihood of capsize. 'Wasn't 1976 bad enough', you might say. True, but no one is going to stop the search for performance and therefore we must find another solution. The number of capsizes, the conditions and the size of craft involved in 1976, were totally unexpected by all concerned. Self-righting theories have existed for years and the only reason that they have not been put into practice was the belief that they were not needed. The view that multihulls, and tris in particular, were never capsized by sea conditions alone was widely held and appeared to be confirmed by vast numbers of multihull voyages all over the world. We were quite wrong but I do believe that the long arm of coincidence had something to do with so many coming to grief in one year.

The incentive is now there to solve the problems of survival in an upturned multihull, and self-righting. Survival alone requires only the planning of stores, dry clothing, a habitable space above the waterlevel within the upturned hull and a ventilation/look-out hatch. Our new boats, like the new *Three Legs of Mann*, have these features built in.

Self-righting is a practical possibility for all multihulls. Time and money is needed for experiment and the final solution will mean some extra gear—but not necessarily all that much. Obviously this is a personal view but it is one I expect to prove in the not too distant future. The average multihull is as stable the wrong way up as it is the right way up, but because the stability is in the form of entrapped air which can be released, the problem is not necessarily as difficult as it might at first appear. A combination of flooding sealed compartments and inflatable buoyancy are likely to be used in the final arrangement.

With the solution to this problem the multihull becomes, without question, the safest craft afloat as well as the most comfortable and best performer.

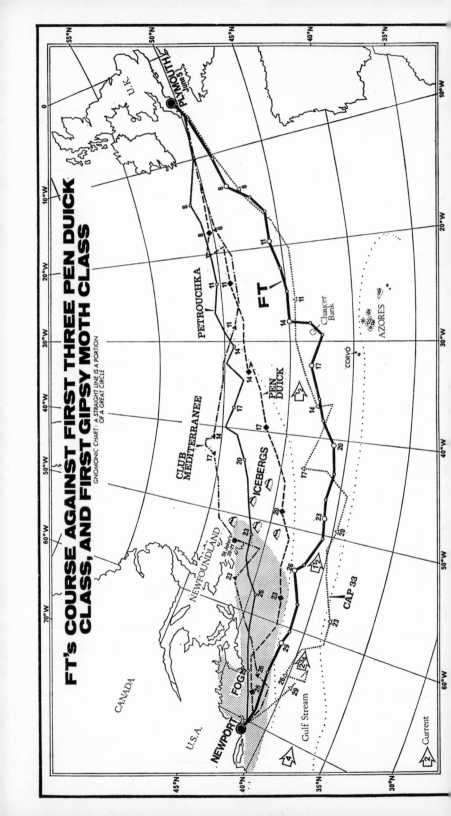

FT's COURSE AGAINST FIRST THREE PEN DUICK CLASS, AND FIRST GIPSY MOTH CLASS

GNOMONIC CHART : A STRAIGHT LINE IS A PORTION OF A GREAT CIRCLE